Contents

AFFECTIVE
TEACHING

Lynne Rompelman

University Press of America,® Inc.
Lanham · New York · Oxford

Copyright © 2002 by
University Press of America,® Inc.
4720 Boston Way
Lanham, Maryland 20706
UPA Acquisitions Department (301) 459-3366

12 Hid's Copse Rd.
Cumnor Hill, Oxford OX2 9JJ

Library of Congress Cataloging-in-Publication Data

Rompelman, Lynne.
Affective teaching / Lynne Rompelman.
p.   cm
Includes bibliographical references.
1. Affective education. 2. Effective teaching.
3. Active learning. I. Title.

LB1072 .R66 2002   2002023137 CIP

ISBN 0-7618-2268-2 (paperback : alk. ppr.)

☉™ The paper used in this publication meets the minimum
requirements of American National Standard for Information
Sciences—Permanence of Paper for Printed Library Materials,
ANSI Z39.48—1984

Preface

We had been discussing diversity in an educational psychology class. I had mentioned to the students how surprised I was to learn that Slavin (1997) felt it was necessary to write that one characteristic of an effective teacher is fairness of treatment for <u>all</u> students. I thought that was understood, a given. After a discussion of differences in learning styles, ability levels, religions, etc. of students, one of my prospective teachers raised his hand and asked, "You mean, if I have a student of a different religion in my class, I need to respect that student?" I really wanted to respond, but I was afraid that my immediate answer would be a bit sarcastic. Fortunately, I didn't need to comment. Other students in the class seemed almost as shocked as I, and they very freely shared their opinions on the need to respect student differences.

Reflecting on this situation, I came to realize that we cannot assume that all people are taught basic rules of civility as some of us have learned in the Golden Rule. We, as professors, cannot assume that even the most obvious is understood. We need to disseminate knowledge within a humanistic, Rogerian framework, modeling appropriate social skills as we teach. We need to understand students' individual needs and design our teaching strategies around those needs. This is necessary in order to engage students most effectively in their own learning.

This book is about the affective domain and how it is an important component of learning at all levels. It includes a summary of the educational literature regarding affective teachers, affective strategies, and the affective educational setting. The book concludes with a question of practical significance, "How am I doing as an affective instructor?"

Historically, research on the affective domain primarily involved elementary and graduate students. I hope that this collection will enhance that body of literature by including voices of undergraduate students. This is information that may be implemented not only at the undergraduate level, but also at any level. Perhaps, these chapters will also stimulate further research into the affective domain.

I have a vested interest in this book. This investigation into the research is for those teachers who might enhance their instruction by an update in educational literature regarding the affective domain. There are many teachers (including me) with lifetime teaching certificates who have never been required to enroll in an educational psychology class, where information on the affective domain is appropriately presented. In attempting to generate a willingness to incorporate new strategies for teaching, I am also hoping to squelch responses from teachers that I have received as a parent of four school-aged children: "It is not my responsibility to motivate your child...", "I've been doing this for twenty years...", "It would be better for you to promote your child to the next grade rather than expect us to individualize work for her..."--to name a few.

Three individuals contributed significantly to the early planning of this book. I acknowledge the late Dr. Peter Becker and Dr. Tim Krenzke (of Concordia University-River Forest) and Dr. Joel Heck (of CU-Austin) for their support of this project.

L.R.

PART 1--WHAT DO WE KNOW ABOUT THE AFFECTIVE DOMAIN?

Learning is either a change in behavior due to experience or a change in mental events due to experience. The difference of perspective in the theories of learning lies in the focus of the definition, whether learning results from a change in observable behaviors or results from a change in mental associations. Most psychologists support one or the other of the two major theoretical perspectives--either the behaviorist or the cognitive--in their definitions of learning. The behavioral or psychomotor domain involves students' sensations or physical responses to stimuli, observable behaviors. The cognitive domain focuses on thinking and memory as processes of learning. A third domain of learning, the affective, is often described by the way in which the emotions of the individual influence his or her learning. The impact of this domain on learning is often overlooked or misunderstood.

The domain of emotions is sometimes regarded as a distraction to learning. However, affect, or the feelings or emotions that influence the completion of an act, impacts learning significantly. For example, when students complete a task, they also discern whether they like the task. Mood influences problem solving and information retrieval; one student may learn better under pressure, especially when studying for an exam, while the same pressure might paralyze another student. It is very difficult to separate affect from observable actions and from cognition. Anxiety is the form of affect that most researchers study. Anxiety either facilitates or interferes with performance on certain tasks, and it also distracts students, blocking effective cognitive processing. Teachers who understand the relationship among behavior, cognition, and affect are able to capitalize on this knowledge in order to engage students in learning. Students who recognize their feelings about a certain topic, for example, are those students who remember the topic more readily. Topics presented within an affective framework become very real, very relevant in students' lives. Affective teaching moves beyond a cognitive presentation toward students' active participation in their own learning.[1] Another way of presenting the overlap of the three domains of learning is by taking a look at the learning process, itself. Affective teachers understand student attitudes and focus on their needs when preparing to teach. Seeking an optimal change in perception, affective teachers attempt to stimulate students. At the same time students are asked how they feel about (involvement in) certain activities. These activities may be adjusted to accommodate students' feelings, which definitely impact their involvement. To check for competency in a particular skill area is the final loop of the learning process. Being effective at something that is valued is an ultimate goal for both students and teachers. Within this learning process, affective teachers focus on the needs of students. They also identify stimulating factors of the activity and employ these factors as a means of fulfilling student needs, a primary objective in teaching. Affective teachers highlight the interesting and relevant aspects within any presentation of content. Students, in response, engage in their own learning. Their thinking and acting are influenced by their attitudes or feelings.

Bloom, Krathwohl, and Masia (1956) divided educational objectives into the psychomotor, cognitive, and affective domains; a taxonomy for each domain was developed. When one compares Bloom's taxonomy of the affective domain to his taxonomy of the cognitive domain, an overlap of the goals is evident. The taxonomy of educational objectives pertinent to the affective domain, or the domain of emotional response, according to Bloom (1964) includes the following:

1. Receiving--attending to something in the environment; for example, a student's interest is piqued because the instructor has asked, "What would *you* do in this particular situation?"

2. Responding--new behavior is a result of an experience; the affective teacher will engage students in their own learning. Responses may be as simple as body language. Even if a student displays negative body language--a shaking of the head in response to a comment the teacher makes--this shaking of the head reflects engagement of the student in learning.

3. Valuing--a decision is made to become involved in or committed to a particular behavior; this valuation is a step beyond responding because it is a student's response that frames future action. For example, a student may realize some degree of intrigue in a concept that the instructor has presented. Worth or value is, then, ascribed to a particular stimulus.

4. Organization/Integration--a prioritization of a new value becomes an important part of one's set of values; to use a Piagetian term, affective teachers will expect students to *accommodate* new information into an already existent mental scheme in order to enhance learning.

Any dissonant information, that which contradicts one's belief system, will have to be "filtered", or integrated into a hierarchical system that, in turn, influences behavior. For example, if a student is faced with a moral dilemma, he or she will have to "sort" values and behave according to a cognitive evaluation of a situation. This, most definitely, is an example of the overlapping of the cognitive and affective domains.

5. Characterization by value--behavior is displayed that is consistent with a new value. Practice of integration of values, for example, in a response paper strengthens particular values until they become a part of one's personality.

This taxonomy of the affective domain frames inner growth once "a person grows aware of, and then adopts attitudes, principles, codes, and sanctions that support value judgments and guide behavior."[2] Affective behaviors are expressed in interests, attitudes, and values; Bloom et al. attempt to describe a continuum ordering and relating different kinds of affective behavior based on objectives dealing with these interests, attitudes, and values.

Bloom's taxonomy of educational objectives of the cognitive domain includes knowledge, comprehension, application, analysis, synthesis, and evaluation. These stages of cognition are enhanced with simultaneous reference to the affective domain; cognitive lessons become more relevant when attention is given to feelings attached to learning activities. Students master information more quickly when it is directly tied to their lives' experiences and when it is of practical use. Learning is not just the transmission of information from one person to another. It is "bundled in affect," influencing behavior. Many educators believe that goals of the two domains--the cognitive and the affective, in particular--should be equally stressed in teaching.

There is a picture book by Albert Cullum (1971) that should be read by every (prospective) teacher. This book is "dedicated to all of those grown-ups who, as children, died in the arms of compulsory education." The book is entitled, <u>The Geranium on the Window Sill Just Died But Teacher You Went Right On</u>; it is a reflection of the teacher who believes that teaching is the mere attempt to transmit knowledge. "Teacher, give me back my 'I'! You promised, teacher, you promised if I was good you'd give it back. You have so many 'I's in the top drawer of your desk. You wouldn't miss mine."[3]

Although our culture acknowledges that emotions exist, it,

historically, has not placed great value on the importance of emotions in learning. However, highly respected neuroscientists LeDoux, Pert, Kagan, Damasio and Damasio "emerged with important research (mid-1980s) that helped to show that emotions drive attention, create meaning, and have their own memory pathways." The researchers concluded, "You can't get more related to learning than that".[4] This, in fact, is the framework for brain-compatible learning--an offshoot of modern brain research. This symbiotic relationship between the cognitive and the affective domains is a focal point in Part 1 of this book.

    Educational literature identifies numerous definitions of "affective" as it is used in the phrase, "affective learning experience". Affective teaching reflects the personal, caring nature of the classroom teacher which enhances the need-fulfillment of students. Affective teaching "is purposive, discovery-based, and action-oriented. It touches mind, heart, and soul."[5] The caring teacher takes into consideration the feelings, values, attitudes, and self-concepts of students. It is fitting, therefore, to discuss teachers and their caring relationships with students in order to understand their influence on student engagement in learning. The affective teacher is described in Chapter 1 of this book. Chapter 2--Affective Instruction, and Chapter 3--Affective Educational Settings conclude Part I. Each of these chapters is written by an educational psychologist, therefore each is heavily dependent on the educational literature regarding the affective domain as well as on examples drawn directly from the classroom.

Notes

1. Jensen, *Teaching with the Brain in Mind*, 71-81.
2. Hamachek, *Human Dynamics in Psychology and Education: Selected Readings*, 379.
3. Cullum, *The Geranium on the Window Sill Just Died But Teacher You Went Right On*, 54.
4. Jensen, op cit., 72.
5. Gallos, "On the Art of Teaching Management," 446.

References

Cullum, A. (1971). *The Geranium on the Window Sill Just Died But Teacher You Went Right On.* Belgium: Harlin Quist.
Gallos, J. "On the Art of Teaching Management," <u>Journal of Management</u>

Education, 21, 4, 446.

Hamachek, D. (1972). *Human Dynamics in Psychology and Education: Selected Readings.* Boston, Massachusetts: Allyn and Bacon.

Jensen, E. (1998). *Teaching with the Brain in Mind.* Alexandria, VA: Association for Supervision and Curriculum Development.

CHAPTER 1–AFFECTIVE TEACHERS

There is a humorous, meaningful story that I like to read to all of my students during the first week of classes. It is entitled <u>The Teacher from the Black Lagoon</u> (Thaler, 1989). The colorful pictures of teachers portray anything other than what one would describe as an affective teacher; Mrs. Jones is seen carrying a whip. Mrs. Green breathes fire and claws the blackboard. It is only at the end of the story when the students learn about a character who embodies affectiveness–a warm, caring, nurturing teacher. She does not carry a whip, nor does she breathe fire. In fact, she hugs her students.

An affective teacher personalizes the learning experience. She focuses on students' needs and presents information in such a way that it is tied to these individual needs; it is relevant information. The affective teacher stimulates students. He concerns himself with guaranteeing a positive student attitude toward learning. (This attitude is not only a perception, but it is a personal judgment that influences behavior in the classroom.) The affective teacher motivates students. S/he listens, attends, gets involved, and displays positive regard for others. These affective descriptors are echoed throughout educational literature which is replete with definitions of affective teachers.

The Summary Report by the National Commission on Teaching and America's Future (1996) begins with the following goal: "By the year 2006, America will provide all students in the country with what should be their educational birthright: access to competent, **CARING** (author's boldface), and qualified teachers."[1] When asked in a pilot study to define "affective" as in "affective teachers," teachers responded in the following manner:

those who...

teach with care and concern
use the discovery method
incorporate hands-on experiences
encourage active engagement in the learning process
focus on the humanistic, emotional sphere
deal with students' problems in positive ways
cause students to feel good about themselves and about their
    achievements
discuss feelings, values education

show sensitivity by meeting students' needs
influence, modify behavior
teach other than at the cognitive level
develop heart interactions
educate at a developmentally appropriate level
deal with a student's well-being[2]

Tomorrow's Teachers (1986), the report of the Holmes Group–deans of education departments of universities across the country–states that teachers need to be in-serviced not only in subject matter areas, but also in human relations. Tomorrow's Teachers includes the following:

Teachers must lead a life of the mind. They must be reflective and thoughtful-persons who seek to understand so they may clarify for others, persons who can go to the heart of the matter.

The development of desirable professional dispositions can be acquired in settings where they are regularly acted out. Creating and sustaining a communal setting respectful of individual differences and group membership where learning is valued, engagement is nurtured, and interests are encouraged requires more than a set of identifiable skills. The successful transmission of these attitudes and values is more a function of the teachers' dispositions and beliefs that come to imbue the classroom culture.[3]

The Holmes Group asks educators to frame their instruction of skills within an affective structure. Educators need to integrate core studies, the substantive, with the technical, personal, and social (Joyce, 1990). This request is based on the Holmes Group's understanding of a place within teaching for love and commitment to social improvement (Joyce, 1990; Bredo, 1990). Social improvement, of which the Holmes Group speaks, involves an understanding of one's responsibility as a citizen.

Critical democracy, as drawn from John Dewey's The Public and Its Problems (1927), implies participation in the values of private or public social life. Individual values, such as cooperation and civic responsibility, balance the scale between individuality and community. Goodman (1989) states that education helps in establishing this balance. It is the affective teacher who frames an individual's understanding of the opposition between personal advancement and responsibility to the good of the community for the sake of sustaining critical democracy. For Dewey, this teacher encourages free inquiry and the virtues of being willing to communicate, being open-minded, and being respectful (Gouinlock, 19878). Democratic habits are the result of participation in the community, an aim of education, according to Dewey.

A "connectionist" perspective is suggested as the framework within which democratic ideals are in focus. This perspective binds an individual to all other living things on earth. Within this framework of positive relationships among school administrators, teachers, and students, the foundational elements of a critical democracy–social bonding, respect, caring, and responsibility–emerge. Educational reformers, those proponents of the concept of a critical democracy, prefer this connectionist perspective to the teacher-centered, didactic approach when analyzing instructional effectiveness (Goodman, 1989).

As I write about this connectionist perspective, I recall an incident involving an elementary teacher and one of my children. Without notice, my parents came to visit, and they offered to watch my younger children when I went to visit the eldest in the classroom. I had been promising her a visit as well as a shared lunch. Following protocol, I stopped in the school's office to announce my visit. I apologized for "no notice"; I explained the surprise visit of my parents to the school principal. The principal went to my daughter's classroom to talk with her teacher.

I was expecting him to say, "Have fun" or something of that sort when he returned. Instead, he said, "The teacher would like you to return another day. She would like to do her best for you." Aghast, I replied, "I expect her to do her best for my daughter every day!" Rather insistent at this point, I was able to visit my daughter in the classroom. I sat at my daughter's desk with her, and we shared lunch in the cafeteria.

The connectionist perspective prescribes a positive, working relationship among all of the people who care for students–between teachers and parents, in particular. A connection or a network of support enhances a student's participation in learning. Parents and teachers working together model the positive relationship of which Goodman speaks. This positive relationship is also reflective of learning within a communal setting that is respectful of individual differences; the Holmes Group suggests the creation of this setting in order to nurture engagement in learning.

In 1944, Edwards spoke of the importance of redirecting education for the purpose of transmitting "ideas, knowledge, values, and skills constituting the capital of human experience within a democratic society".[4] Edwards continued that although education should be concerned with the transmission of culture, it was also to focus on the development of personality. "And if the individual [were] to make a satisfactory adjustment to his culture, the school needed to provide the individual with concrete experiences which [would] develop in him the values, motivations, desires, sensitivities, and the skills which his society demanded." [5] The school was to function as a critic of social values and processes. A goal of affective education was to enhance the freedom and responsibility of each student within a democratic society. "For a democratic society to flourish and increase in health and realistic productivity, as a society and also in terms of the welfare of the individual, its members must learn how to combine freedom with responsibility; their combination is crucial for the continued health of society."[6]

Bronfenbrenner (1986) echoes Edwards's ideas. He states that the school "is in the best position of all U.S. institutions to initiate and strengthen links that support children and adolescents." Within a caring curriculum, students not only learn about caring, but they also engage in it. They learn "'citizenship': what it means to be a member of society, how to behave toward others, and what one's responsibilities are to the community and to the nation."[7]

Arnstine (1990) suggests that prepared teachers, in any environment, are those who succeed in the attainment of educational aims–rational and caring persons. These teachers, themselves, need to be rational and caring models for their students. Dispositions to be rational and caring cannot be postponed; these dispositions need to be cultivated.

Although there are far more caring teachers in the classroom than the uncaring, it always seems to be the uncaring teachers who are remembered. I remember too many non-affective teachers in my children's educational careers. I know a fifth grade teacher who is a computer wizard. Unfortunately, he treats his students only as numbers, except for the handful who excel in all academic areas. At the end of every week he staples a computerized checklist into the assignment notebooks of those students who are missing work. When I asked my daughter if the teacher ever discussed this computerized list with her, she replied, "Never". During many evening homework sessions, I was really at a loss as to how to help my daughter; often, she didn't even know how to "fix the problem."

I met with another daughter's teachers during the middle of her seventh grade year. My concern was that she was quite bored with her schoolwork even though she was doing extremely well. After a forty minute discussion during which I asked the teachers to challenge her, the teachers jointly stated that it would be better to move my daughter on to the eighth grade than to ask them to individualize work for her.

My son has always been a good speller. Wondering why he always had to memorize "those easy lists of words," he asked if I thought there was something else he could do to learn spelling words. We brain stormed and I shared our suggestions with my son's teacher. The teacher's response was, "Mrs. Rompelman, it is not my job to motivate your child. I've been teaching spelling this same way for twenty years." I politely suggested that if this had been his method for so long, perhaps it was time to change, especially to meet the needs of his student!

(Please know that it is not just these single examples by which I have identified these particular teachers as non-affective. This is just a sampling of some of the experiences I have had with my children that are seemingly reflective of a lack of care for my students' needs.)

"Caring is surely an essential aspect of education in a free society...".[8]

The Affective Teacher

As early as 1896, a study by Kratz of 2000 school children identified descriptors of the best teachers students had ever had. One of the characteristics most often identified was kindness (Gazda, 1977). Likewise, in 1934, Hart asked high school students to describe their best teachers. The "human" and "friendly" teacher was the favorite teacher of the students.

To summarize eight studies completed between 1900 and 1946, Evans (1962) stated, "Children apparently know quite clearly what they like and what they dislike in their teachers":

Affective teachers are kind, friendly, cheerful, patient, helpful, fair, have a sense of humor, show an understanding of human problems and maintain order...They are not sarcastic, likely to ridicule, or those who punish to secure discipline. They do not fail to provide for the needs of individual pupils.[9]

Instruction

An affective teacher integrates the instruction of identifiable skills in a caring manner. He or she "cultivates dispositions that are available in activities perceived by students to be purposeful."[10] Bullough (1989) states that the affective professional is one who respects and learns from his students while providing effectively for them. Reflective teachers, or those who learn from their own experiences, seem to be those memorable teachers whose characteristics are remembered long after a student leaves the classroom (Johnson & Prom-Jackson, 1986).

The affective teacher perceives that the student is able to learn; this is a premise, the teacher's philosophy of education. "Teachers who see students as unable are defeated before they begin and their teaching is likely to devolve into spiritless plodding toward hopeless goals or attacks upon students for their perversity, apathy, or stupidity."[11]

The affective teacher communicates instruction effectively and displays a sense of humor. The teacher is firm, yet fair–not only in grading, but in disciplining, as well. The affective teacher knows his or her subject area well and is able to disseminate information in a personalized fashion. This personalization, involving the questioning of students ("What would you do in this situation?") and the incorporation of students' names in discussion, to name a few examples, makes the information more relevant and easier to remember.

Relationships with Students

Interpersonal skills of teachers are judged by students as important, if not more important, than cognitive skills. A 1991 poll by Elam, Gallup, and Rose revealed that if the public were given the chance to hire teachers, 77% would select a person with a high degree of expertise in a particular academic subject who also demonstrated a talent for teaching, as opposed to 26% who would select a person with a high degree of expertise or knowledge in a particular academic subject, only. Skills in verbal and non-verbal communication can be perfected, and these skills frame the teacher/student relationship (Morrison, 1983).

An affective teacher establishes rapport with students which promotes engagement in learning and positive self-esteem (Good & Brophy, 1971, 1973). He or she supports student endeavors. Understanding the uniqueness of the individual enables the teacher to accept and appreciate the differences among students. "Understanding uniqueness is also helpful in dealing with such pressing problems as desegregation, ethnic differences, and the demands of youth for greater respect and autonomy." Combs continues,

Teachers who exude positive beliefs about students are, thus, likely to find their beliefs confirmed in greater student interest, involvement, commitment, expenditures of effort, higher achievement, and fewer discipline problems. Under such conditions, everyone wins.[12]

Effectiveness

An affective teacher is an effective teacher, according to Arnstine (1990). Effective schools are comprised of affective teachers, those who interact more with students, have friendlier classrooms, and have higher expectations of students.[13]

Jackson and Getzels (1971) find an empirical linkage between school effectiveness and dissatisfaction in youth. The greatest school dissatisfaction is seen in extreme ability groups of students. Rigid structure and a traditional curriculum are seen as factors of dissatisfaction within the schools, especially in regard to adolescents' needs for "self-control, responsibility, freedom, and relevancy." These needs may be met by "lively teachers" who foster individual growth.[14]

Fostering Growth

Effective persons, affective teachers are healthy in physical, emotional, and intellectual senses (Carkhuff, 1977). Not only are affective teachers healthy individuals, but they also realize the basic drive of an organism toward health. Combs (1982) speaks of the individual's insatiable, active drive toward growth. Many professions, including teaching, are predicated on the individual's need for fulfillment. This need-fulfillment is not only of the physical self, but it is of the larger self-concept. According to Combs, the human organism is "ripe" for molding into a productive member of society. Behavioral, intellectual, and emotional capacities are almost limitless. Also, the uniqueness of individuals contributes to the welfare of the whole of society. This view of the unique individual, as actively growing toward his/her potential, has many implications for teachers. The affective/effective practitioner must be aware of student needs. "Before education can make a difference in the lives of students it must meet their needs."[15]

Summary

Johnson and Prom-Jackson (1986) find that affective characteristics of teachers are those traits that set them apart as influential persons. Ferguson and Thomas (1987) identify other descriptors of affective teachers: approachable, easy to relate to, caring, perceptive, and tolerant. Affective teachers are also labeled "good teachers."[16] They are ever-observant, active listeners who meet students' needs.

Needs of All Students: Rural, Urban, At-Risk

Eitzen (1992) states that society is responsible for many of the problems that students experience. He states that the "system" needs to take blame for social problems. The ever-changing economy may take the credit for the loss of millions of parents' jobs. Wage cuts and concessions are common. The American standard of living is declining. Eitzen also states that changes in the economy impact the dreams of many students for a college education. These economic trends signal downward social mobility. Family and individual self-esteems are affected.

In conjunction with these problems for students created by economic shifts are problems caused by stress, depression, and alcoholism. Intolerable behavior may characterize students who are rejected by peers. These rejected students may also be involved in "gang membership, confrontation with and disobedience to authority, and experimentation with drugs and sex."[17]

The changing economy is only one aspect of the system that impacts students. Changing racial landscapes, changing government policy, and changing family structure create additional contemporary issues for the student (Eitzen, 1992). The implication for the teacher to acquire or enhance affective qualities seems evident; if the teacher were to develop a single affective quality, such as active listening, he or she would be able to help students who are coping with contemporary issues. This affiliative nature may be even more imperative for the instructors who work with students transitioning from adolescence into early adulthood.

Arnstine (1990) said that a prepared and caring, or affective teacher, succeeds in realizing the attainment of educational goals within any environment. In 1938, Rosecrance reinforced this idea in his research. However, he argued that there is greater potential to enable one to understand the whole child within a rural setting than within an urban setting. A more personalized relationship may be developed within a rural situation involving fewer students. Although urban settings may not be as conducive to individualized attention, there may be more community resources available there to enhance the teacher-student relationship, according to Rosecrance. In both types of schools, rural and urban, Rosecrance (1938) suggests the employment of a counselor as a mentor for teachers in order to most effectively meet students' needs.

Rosecrance studied more than 2500 students from around the country; these students revealed that they looked to their teachers as their primary sources of problem resolution. The needs of the students, all students, were to be a priority for teachers. The significant events in students' school days seemed to occur in the everyday experiences that molded and developed their lives (Rosecrance, 1938).

With growing numbers of at-risk students enrolled in schools, today, it seems even more important for teachers to be able to develop an ethic of caring (McLaughlin & Talbert, 1990). According to McLaughlin and Talbert, at-risk students are motivated by personal bonds established with adults. Interpersonal accountability is a type of contract between students and teachers. That teachers are able to establish this rapport through a "contract" with students reflects an understanding of multiculturalism and an understanding of national survival (Trachtenberg, 1990). "Programs that effectively reach [at-risk] students are those that simultaneously address the many problems these [students] face at home as well as at school."[18] Almost all students who are identified as "at-risk" require individual attention. Healthy, positive relationships between teachers and students of all cultural backgrounds may engage students in their learning environment. Interaction and support in programs that build on individual strengths may yield more immediate successes for students (Sheingold, 1991).

Students respond best to "teachers who are warm, friendly, immediate, approachable, affiliative, and fostering of close, professionally appropriate personal relationships."[19] Students appreciate questions regarding their personal lives. A humanistic approach to teaching focuses on the individual needs of students. Is there a better way to learn about your students' needs other than to ask them?

Student teachers maintain images of teachers as guides and friends (Weinstein, 1989). Affiliative teacher messages seem to return to full circle; teachers share on the basis of the rewards offered to them. Human communication, reciprocal in nature, appeals to similar messages from others.

There are some studies which focus on characteristics of "good" and "poor" teachers, according to students' perspectives. Johnson (1975) asked students, "What makes a good teacher?" and "What is the most helpful thing a teacher ever said to you or did for you?" "Good" and "helpful" teachers were those who offered encouragement. Positive descriptors of affective teachers that were found by Johnson echoed responses that Andersen and Andersen (1987) collected years later.

College students rated the affiliative nature of teachers highly. Student instructional ratings were analyzed, and a main effect relationship was found between personality and teaching (Murray, Paunonen, Sampo, & Rushton, 1990). Teachers excelling in all types of courses, on the basis of instruction, were found to be friendly, supportive, strict, and demanding. These master teachers were effective not only in lecture but also in seminar formats. They developed interpersonal skills and were able to motivate both the capable and less capable students.

Nel Noddings (1987) sees the nation neglecting its students in the instruction of care or of relation. Psyches are prepared for threatened stances by rivals, enemies. Noddings discusses relational ethics and offers methods of developing caring relationships; the author sees the role of the effective teacher as one of care-giving. "Teachers must find ways to be with their students–to talk with them (not at them) about their lives and about great intellectual ideas, to solve problems with them, and to share cultural delights."[20]

I recall a counseling relationship with a second grade boy that developed over a two-year period. The student had been referred to me, the elementary counselor, a few weeks after his mother had died. When Jimmy returned to school after the funeral, he was not able to concentrate very well on any of his schoolwork. It seemed that my immediate goal was to just listen, to learn what Jimmy was thinking and feeling. Most of our sessions were devoted to just talking–about everything! We played in the sandbox while we talked. We played catch in the gym while we talked. I listened to Jimmy's problems at home and to his problems at school. We brain stormed solutions to the problems. With a regular check on Jimmy's progress, I saw his despondent behavior wane; Jimmy seemed to flourish once again.

I remained an elementary counselor for several years within the district that Jimmy attended. Then I returned to the classroom. Imagine my surprise when Jimmy walked into my sixth grade! I will never forget meeting with Jimmy and his father at the first conference of the year. They both thanked me for my earlier help. It seems that I was able to support Jimmy at a time when he most needed a caring hand. I attribute Jimmy's growth–both academic and social–to the very simple skill of active listening.

In a Rogerian fashion, Easterly (1984) refers to the affective teacher as one who is mentally, physically, and emotionally well. Coining the title of Sheehy's (1984) book, Easterly defines a pathfinder as one who is willing to risk change. A pathfinder also has capacity for loving, and she or he possesses androgynous characteristics. Pathfinders, themselves, report self-fulfillment especially within a supportive network of family, friends, cohorts, and relatives (Easterly, 1984). It is not only evident that an effective teacher exhibits general well-being, but also the effective teacher shares positive affect. Greater confidence in the teacher and thus, in the wisdom he imparts is a classroom benefit of shared positive affect (Andersen & Andersen, 1987).

In an informal survey (Rompelman, 1996)[21], undergraduate

students provided the following responses in regard to a question about descriptors of affective teachers:

friendly and outgoing
positive when it comes to expectations of the class
understanding of students' needs
able to treat each person as an individual
good listeners
ones who smile
patient
able to remove bias of race and religion from the atmosphere
non-judgmental
ones with a sense of humor
enthusiastic
willing to personally interact with students
approachable
genuine, especially in regard to caring about students
concerned more about students' needs than about the amount
        of material presented
reflecting an attitude of wanting to teach and of enjoying
        their teaching
sensitive to the needs of the students
respectful of students
able to assume an affective stance outside of the classroom–
        in the hallway, e.g.
comfortable in sharing their faith, their beliefs
willing to offer one-on-one help

One suggestion that was offered by a student in this survey seems to summarize the aforementioned descriptors: "I feel that the faculty members are affective teachers in that they genuinely care about the students. If I could offer one suggestion it would be to remind all the faculty members that we are individuals and unique, not nameless faces that they see every day."

A list of descriptors equally as long may be presented regarding teachers' adjectives for the affective personality. These data were collected during a pilot study (Rompelman, 1992):

warm

able to express emotions easily
concerned for the well-being of the student
flexible
respectful
willing to take time for students
aware of social issues
willing to listen
emotionally stable
caring
open
loving
dedicated
desirous of putting students first
sympathetic
understanding
polite
patient
possessing a sense of humor
creative
not critical of others
not afraid to act on a problem
sensitive
truthful
compassionate
confident
good communicator
sincere
positive
firm
friendly
supportive
encouraging
goal-oriented
tender
not afraid to make and admit errors
willing to spend hours devising lessons
observant
responsive
mature
non-judgmental

These descriptors were offered by teachers when asked, "What are some characteristics of a teacher who uses affective teaching techniques?"

Educational literature definitely supports these student and teacher comments regarding the affective teacher. Warmth, empathic understanding, unconditional positive regard, and genuineness are critical factors in studies of students (Bayer, 1986). Dacey (1986) concurs with these adjectives as is evident in responses he collected from adolescents. He asked, "How would you change your teachers?" Common responses were: "Try to get to know us as individuals. When we feel like you know us, we feel we can trust you. Try not to be prejudiced, and don't pick favorites. Don't punish the majority because the minority is misbehaving. Respect our personal rights more. Trust us more."[22]

Carl Rogers (1959) refers to the classroom teacher as a therapist who cares for students as separate persons within an environment in which significant learning may occur. Empathy is a critical characteristic of the therapist. That the therapist/teacher is able to understand the world of the student from the inside is basic to establishing rapport. The caring and acceptance of the therapist for the student must be communicated in order to enhance the development of a positive self-concept.

According to Rogers, teachers need to realize their own attitudes and need to accept their own feelings. Congruence implies being a "real" person. Unconditional positive regard and empathy are traits of teachers that cement relationships with not only the students, but also with the parents and others of the community. The affective/effective teachers' concern is the self-actualizing tendency of students, or helping them to realize their potentials. "The hypothesis upon which [the teachers] would build is that students who are in real contact with life problems wish to learn, want to grow, seek to find out, hope to master, desire to create. [They] would see [their] function as that of developing such a personal relationship with students and such a climate in classrooms, that these natural tendencies could come to their fruition."[23] Rogers sees significant learning in schools as a function of an individual's decisions in light of his relationship with an accepting, empathetic, real teacher (Rogers, 1959).

The "real" teacher, who Rogers portrays, has a general awareness of child, adolescent, or adult development as minimal preparation for teaching. As well as possessing this basic knowledge, the teacher needs to assume an affective stance; she needs to be the care giver. This position may be attained by:

1. Studying human relations;
2. Studying the techniques by which relations are created–projection,

association/dissociation, etc; and
3. Modeling the "better way"–educating the heart.[24]

One implication of modeling the "better way"–"heart interactions" between teachers and students–is the importance of continued enhancement of teachers' learning and practice of affective strategies. Advanced courses for teachers to learn affective strategies as well as a program of colleagues as mentors may be established. Teachers helping teachers–through observation and feedback–may verify the practicality and effectiveness of certain affective strategies. Observations of another teacher using affective techniques may encourage one to become more affective herself. A regulated or monitored follow-up study of teachers receiving in-service training in the affective domain is needed in order to offer support to those who wish to become a part of an entire staff who can effectively meet students' needs.

Some universities (such as UW-Platteville) have offered summer seminars that focus on students' needs. Workshops are offered for educators on the following topics: advising, interaction, communication, identification of students' needs for growth, and teaching to those needs.

When I worked with a team of colleagues who attended a workshop for transescents, or those transitioning into adolescence, I gathered invaluable information to help me as a middle school teacher. My colleagues and I brain stormed different activities to meet our adolescents' needs. The plan was to involve the students in activities which were not a part of the regular curriculum–activities equally important for learning, but different, exciting connections to life, reality.

One activity that actually evolved into an annual career day, included members of the community who shared their expertise with the students. Students had a choice of four "career sessions" to attend. Some of the more popular sessions were those led by the cosmetologist, the train buff, the gourmet cook, and the yoga instructor. Each student was expected to participate and to ask questions of the leaders. There were some sessions that were difficult to conclude because the students had so many questions! The hands-on activities were evaluated by a majority of the students as, "Awesome!"

The planning, development and implementation of this project were to open lines of communication and interaction among students, teachers, parents, and other community members. Partnerships were encouraged to strengthen the educational process. Problem-solving, critical thinking, skill development, and group process activities were in focus in order to enhance educational achievement.

Training for teachers in human relations by such means can only increase empathy for students (Redman, 1977). Strategies of values clarification may become one aspect of "adventurous teaching" (Jackson, 1988). Socialization processes of teachers may be redesigned to focus on "other orientation." Strategies during "encounter" and "change" and "acquisition" stages of the socialization process of novice teachers may be incorporated and practiced within teacher preparation programs. Apprenticeships and mentoring situations of novices with veteran teachers may enhance the socialization process.

Advisory program development is another means through which students' needs may be met. Teachers are trained as advisors and students reap the benefits from "well-planned, effectively delivered advisory programs" (Ayres, 1994). Although Ayres believes that many teachers fear dealing with students in the affective domain because of their lack of skills and training, the author emphasizes the importance of relationships as the essence of advisories. "Warm, caring, and friendly environments where teachers relate to students on a variety of levels" are prerequisite to engagement in learning.[25]

Prepared teachers, according to Arnstine (1990) are those who are rational and caring. Affective teachers, those who are concerned with care-giving and reciprocity, are those teachers who are "with" their students; they are "talking with them, not at them about their lives, solving problems with them, sharing..." (Rompelman, 1992). Eisner (1983) compares the effective teacher to an artist, to one who must act. "To function as an artist or a craftsperson one must be able to read the ineffable yet expressive messages of classroom life. It requires a level of ... 'educational connoisseurship'–the ability to appreciate what one has encountered."[26] Teachers who relate to students most effectively are those teachers who incorporate affective strategies. Many affective strategies are included in the next chapter, "Affective Instruction."

Notes

1. Report of the National Commission on Teaching, 5.
2. Data were collected in a survey completed by the author in 1992.
3. Holmes Group, *Tomorrow's Teachers*, 54.
4. Edwards, in Henry (Ed.), *National Society for the Study of Education: Adolescence (Part I)*, 195.
5. Henry, op cit., 196.
6. Brown, *Human Teaching for Human Learning: An Introduction to Confluent Education*, 209.

7. Bronfenbrenner, in Feinberg, *The Holmes Group Report and the Professionalization of Teaching,* 167.
8. Feinberg, op cit., 166.
9. Evans, in Gazda, et al., *Human Relations Development,* 9.
10. Arnstine, "Rational and Caring Teachers: Reconstructing Teacher Preparation", 235.
11. Combs, *A Personal Approach to Teaching: Beliefs That Make a Difference",* 29.
12. Combs, op cit., 32-33.
13. Cobb, *Adolescence,* 277.
14. Muuss, *Adolescent Behavior and Society: A Book of Readings,* 361, 374.
15. Combs, op cit., 28.
16. Ferguson and Thomas, "In Celebration of the Teacher", 276.
17. Eitzen, "Problem Students: The Sociocultural Roots", 587.
18. Cobb, op cit., 287.
19. Andersen and Andersen, "Never Smile Until Christmas: Casting Doubt on an Old Myth", 57.
20. Andersen and Andersen, op cit.
21. Data were collected in 1996 by the author; the survey was administered to undergraduate students.
22. Dacey, *Adolescents Today,* 328.
23. Rogers, "Significant Learning: In Therapy and Education", 160.
24. Noddings, op cit., 30.
25. Ayres, "Middle School Advisory Programs: Findings from the Field", 8.
26. Eisner, "The Art and Craft of Teaching", 11.

References

Andersen, J. and P. Andersen (1987). "Never Smile Until Christmas: Casting Doubt on an Old Myth," Journal of Thought, 22, 4.
Arnstine, B. (1990). "Rational and Caring Teachers: Reconstructing Teacher Preparation," Teachers College Record, 92, 2.
Ayres, L. (1994). "Middle School Advisory Programs: Findings from the Field" Leadership, 39, 7.
Bayer, D. (1986). "The Effects of Two Methods of Affective Education on Self-Concept in Seventh Grade Students," The School Counselor, 34, 2.
Bredo, E. (1990). "Contradictions in Teacher Education and Society: A Critical Analysis," Journal of Teacher Education, 41, 2.
Brown, G. (1971). *Human Teaching for Human Learning: An Introduction to Confluent Education.* England: Penguin Books.
Carkhuff, R. (1977). "The Effective Ingredients of Teaching: The Preferred Mode of Helping," Developmental Theory (Minnesota Department of Education), 6.
Cobb, N. (1992). *Adolescence.* California: Mayfield Publishing.

Combs, N. (1982). *A Personal Approach to Teaching: Beliefs that Make a Difference.* Boston: Allyn and Bacon.

Dacey, J. (1986). *Adolescents Today.* Illinois: Scott Foresman.

Dewey, J. (1927). *The Public and Its Problems.* Denver: A. Swallow.

Easterly, J. (1984). "Outstanding Teachers: Pathfinders for the Profession," Action in Teacher Education, 6, 3.

Eitzen, D. (1992). "Problem Students: The Sociocultural Roots," Phi Delta Kappan, 73, 8.

Elam, S., A. Gallup, and L. Rose (1991). "The 23rd Annual Gallup Poll of the Public's Attitudes Toward the Public Schools," Phi Delta Kappan, 73, 1.

Feinberg, W. (1987). "The Holmes Group Report and the Professionalization of Teaching," The Peabody Journal of Education, 88, 3.

Gazda, G., F. Asbury, F. Balzer, W. Childers, and R. Walters (1977). *Human Relations Development.* Boston: Allyn and Bacon.

Good, T. and J. Brophy (April, 1971). "The Self-Fulfilling Prophecy," Today's Education.

Good, T. and J. Brophy (1973). *Looking in Classrooms.* New York: Harper and Row.

Goodman, J. (1980). "Education for Critical Democracy," Journal of Education, 171, 2.

Gouinlock, J. (1987). "Education, Ethics, Politics, and Academic Freedom," Journal of Thought, 22, 3.

Henry, N. (Ed.)(1944). *National Society for the Study of Education: Adolescence (Part I).* Chicago: University of Chicago Press.

Holmes Group (1986). *Tomorrow's Teachers.* Michigan: Holmes Group.

Jackson, P. and J. Getzels (1971). "Psychological Health and Classroom Functioning: A Study of Dissatisfaction with School Among Adolescents" in R. Muuss (Ed.), *Adolescent Behavior and Society: A Book of Readings.* New York: Random House.

Joyce, B. (Ed.)(1990). "Changing School Culture through Staff Development," ASCD Yearbook.

McLaughlin, M. and J. Talbert (1990). "Constructing a Personalized School Environment," Phi Delta Kappan, 72, 3.

Morrison, H. (1983). "Communication and the Teacher-Pupil Relationship," Focus on Learning, 9, 2.

Murray, H., V. Paunonen, and P. Rushton (1990). "Teacher Personality Traits and Student Instructional Ratings in Six Types of University Courses," Journal of Educational Psychology, 82, 2.

National Commission on Teaching and America's Future (1996). *What Matters Most: Teaching for America's Future.* New York: NCTAF.

Noddings, N. (1987). "Creating Rivals and Making Enemies," Journal of Thought, 22, 3.

Redman, G. (1977). "Study of the Relationship of Teacher Empathy for Minority

Persons and Inservice Human Relations Training," Journal of Educational Research, 70, 4.

Rogers, C. (1959). "Significant Learning: In Therapy and Education," Educational Leadership, 16.

Rogers, C. (1969). *Freedom to Learn*. Columbus: Charles Merrill.

Rosecrance, F. (1938). "The Staff Needed for the Development of an Effective Guidance Service," Yearbook of the National Society Study of Education, 37, 1.

Sheingold, K. (1991). "Restructuring for Learning with Technology: The Potential for Synergy," Phi Delta Kappan, 73, 1.

Trachtenberg, S. (1990). "Multiculturalism Can Be Taught Only by Multicultural People," Phi Delta Kappan, 71, 8.

CHAPTER 2
AFFECTIVE INSTRUCTION

An old issue of *The Teaching Professor* defines "great teaching as purposive, discovery-based, and action-oriented. It touches the mind, heart, and soul. It creates genuine opportunities for teacher and student to join in a collaborative search for understanding and direction."[11] This "heart interaction" is one pole or extreme on the learning continuum. Hitler rests at the other end.

I met Hitler, **who chose this name for himself**, when I moved into my sixth grade classroom. He was kind enough to allow me to interview him as I gathered data for my dissertation. Although this particular teacher feels that helping students is a priority, and although he prides himself in getting to know students and how they feel, when he was asked about the students' responses to particular teaching and disciplinary techniques, he responded, "Students don't like to walk into the classroom, instantly shut up, sit in their desks, fold their hands and wait for instruction. They like a little free time in the beginning. When I assume the Adolf Hitler approach whereby I tell kids when they can breathe, they learn pretty quickly. That's the utmost in discipline, but it works." He reported that students react positively to him because they can't "get away with things."

When Hitler's students were interviewed, I wondered whether they would corroborate the teacher's reference to a dictator. Although it seemed that all three students who were interviewed had a positive relationship with the teacher, two reported information about the teacher's routine change in temperament and strictness. One student said that when he entered the classroom, the teacher was "mostly mad because of the class that had just left. [Those students] mostly fool around and the teacher gets mad, and it carries over to our class." Another said that the teacher "needs to cool down, to not be so upset". When I observed the teacher, I recorded several statements that were made to the students: "I usually don't like to compare classes, but my last year's class caught on better in the subject than you...Listen to this explanation and THINK, something that a lot of you don't like to do...Now think. Here's where I have a difficult time with this class. Half of this class should know the answer and you don't. Some of you...if I ask you a question...we talked about this in the teachers' room...you get mixed up. Three-fourths of you got that wrong. I'm not trying to put you down or belittle you. I'm just trying to show you what you can't do."

In closing my interview with the teacher, Hitler proceeded to tell me a story about the "Worst Student of the Month Election." The students would get to elect the worst student within the classroom. (I believe this classification would be based on grades.) That student would then be "taken out on the back forty and shot." Hitler continued, "There is an election every month. It would be desirable to set up a situation whereby the students actually believe that someone is shot so that they learn to toe the mark. I would make arrangements with the school board and with a student and his family, who I know would be out of town for a certain period of time. When the student didn't come back, the others in the classroom would worry and probably act very attentive (sic) to everything I said." He concluded, "I know, though, that the Board probably would not buy into this deal." Wouldn't every administrator love to have this teacher and this philosophy at work in his district? (Actually, upon reading my dissertation, my superintendent asked me to identify Hitler, something I could not do for him.)

Affective instruction?

Several years before I met Hitler, I had been asked by the school superintendent to attend a three-day conference in Ohio. A road trip! Needless to say, I was excited; I had never been asked to represent an entire school district! Here was the deal: Two other colleagues and I would attend the TESA conference in Ohio--all expenses paid. But we would have to drive, and we were obligated to share our knowledge with remaining faculty upon our return. That sounded all right to me.

One hour into the trip, after listening to the "shotgun passenger" read EVERY road sign we passed on the freeway, I was having second thoughts. Luckily, I had the entire back seat; I stretched, covered my head with a pillow and slept a good portion of the day. I awakened to the reading of road signs in Illinois! Never did I ask how far we had yet to go, because I thought that if I actually knew the remaining distance, I would have pulled my hair from my head. OHIO--ten plus hours later! I was never so glad to escape to a hotel room. I was not looking forward to attending this three-day conference.

HOWEVER...The information that I collected and retained from this conference, I can now say, without a doubt, has enhanced my teaching in multitudinous ways. **TESA** stands for Teacher Expectations and Student Achievement. The program is an offshoot of the Equal Opportunity in the Classroom project which began in the 1970s in Los Angeles. This program is not only well-known across the country, but its workshops are also well-attended. There is an extensive body of literature that supports every aspect of its model. Names like Bloom, Good and Brophy, Rogers, and Rosenshine support TESA's premises. Many of these names have also been included in this book's chapters as representative of research in the affective domain. TESA materials are the "brain child" of Mary Martin and Sam Kerman; they are copyrighted by Phi Delta Kappa.[2] The remainder of the information in this chapter needs to be credited to Martin and Kerman; it is a summary of my experience at the Ohio workshop.

The original goal of the Elementary and Secondary Education Act, Title III was "to field test an educational innovation to eliminate or reduce differential treatment in the classroom of children who are poor, culturally different, and/or low achievers." The basic premise of the test is the self-fulfilling prophecy: "teacher behavior toward children for whom low expectations are held tends to be expressive of that low expectation, and increases the probability that the expectation will be fulfilled, and that the child's educational opportunities will be curtailed."[3] Strategies are identified that assist the teacher in meeting the needs of students.

What is so *very* interesting about TESA is that it affords labels for all the good "stuff" that so many of us are incorporating into our teaching at present. We ARE affective teachers. I don't know that there is one teacher who could be identified as totally non-affective, not even Hitler. Many students respected and appreciated Hitler's shotgun approach to teaching. However, TESA informs us all how we can enhance our affective skills. And...it is not difficult! With practice and feedback from colleagues, especially, we can become more affective teachers!

TESA identifies 15 different teacher interactions that are both supportive and motivating in regard to relationships with students. These 15 affective techniques are identified because 1) they are operationally defined; 2) they are observed in typical classrooms; and 3) they have been measured in classrooms. These interactions are divided into three strands: response opportunities, feedback, and personal regard. Each of these interactions is important in its own right; therefore, each is described below. (Please remember that each interaction has a strong research framework. Bibliographic material is available through Phi Delta Kappa.)

1. Equitable Distribution of Response Opportunity--calling on one to answer, demonstrate, affirm, or correct. This interaction is not meant, in any way, to create embarrassment for students. As early as 1914, Horn found

that higher achievers were called upon three times more than lower achievers. There seemed to be several reasons for this: a) teachers do not want to embarrass a student who may not know the answer; b) teachers want the class to hear the correct or most thoughtful response; and c) high quality student performance rewards the teacher's efforts. Good and Brophy found that teachers praise high achievers more often and direct less criticism toward them. When low achievers respond, they receive less praise than higher achievers giving the same response. Response opportunity is defined as "a specific opportunity provided by the teacher for a pupil to respond to a question, recite, read aloud, express an opinion, give a report, do a problem at the board, demonstrate something or to confirm a response by another student."[4]

Robert Slavin suggests in his text, Educational Psychology, that in order to offer equal response opportunity to all students that until we get to know the students well, we should even carry a class list around the room and use check marks each time a student responds. This way we are able to see whether every student is participating, accepting the opportunity to succeed, and thereby learning.

2. Individual Helping--this is a more private interaction between a student and a teacher. Although low achievers require more individual help, they are generally the students who are the least assertive in acquiring it. Individual help may be offered not only during class time and during small group work, but it also may be offered by the teacher during recess, lunch, before and after school times. Educational literature is replete with studies that show that any time spent interacting with a teacher or a tutor is more productive than time spent in independent practice. It may only take a few minutes of "private time" to get a student back on track again.

3. Latency--this is **wait time**. Wait time is the time we offer students to respond to a question. Many have offered suggestions in regard to the length of wait time. I have heard three seconds, five seconds, eight seconds, and ten seconds. We think this is such a simple strategy to adopt. However, wait time can be unbearable--especially in a college classroom. Many times I have to announce in class, "This is wait time", in order to remind myself not to answer my own question. Usually the teacher bends in answering his/her own question because of discomfort. If we recall that it takes a while to trigger information from the memory bank, it only makes sense that if we

allow our students enough time to formulate a reasonable response to a question, they will most likely succeed. I always ask my Ed. Psych. students, "How do you feel when your professor continually answers his/her own questions?" They begin to understand the importance of wait time. If, after waiting an appropriate amount of time, and no one is able to respond, it is wise to simply rephrase the question, or to use more probes. I had a professor who once stated that teachers need to make the question as simple as possible for the students to answer rather than answering themselves. Students may then be praised for their efforts. This, in turn, will reinforce participation and learning.

4. Delving--this interaction includes rephrasing and giving clues. The extent of delving is based on the teacher's awareness of the many styles of student learning. By just repeating a question, a teacher is not delving. This is definitely a form of wait time as it gives students a chance to think and regroup before responding. Delving also enhances the development of higher order thinking skills.

5. Higher Level Questioning--this level of questioning is evident when it requires a student to "do something more than merely remember the answer from reading, previous teacher instruction, or another source. Higher level questions are those that generate
>*an opinion
>*an assessment of facts
>*an evaluation information or ideas
>*an explanation of phenomena
>*discovery of connections among facts
>*an application of previously-learned information to a new situation
>*an organization of information
>*a hypothesis
>*an interpretation of information
>*an explanation of non-literal information as symbolism and irony
>*summaries
>*implications
>*unstated assumptions
>*distinctions between facts and hypotheses
>*inconsistencies
>*a formation of a whole from parts

*logical explanations
*generalizations"[5]

These questioning strategies enhance higher order thinking. It is important to avoid ONE-right-answer questions, whenever possible, especially when the goal is to enhance higher order thinking.

The second strand of affective teaching techniques falls under the FEEDBACK category:

6. Affirm/Correct--information that enables a student to know what the teacher thinks of his/her performance. Students WANT to know what the teacher thinks about them and their work. Research shows that low achieving students usually receive decreased praise or affirmation and even, correction. This is also the case among students of different ethnic backgrounds. Negative, sarcastic responses as feedback are not considered affective. Also, the teacher may involve other students in providing affirmation.

7. Praise of Learning Performance--according to behavioral learning theory, praise is a highly effective strategy to increase the likelihood that an appropriate behavior will be repeated. The literature shows us that high achieving students are usually the ones who are praised the most. On the other hand, low-achieving students are usually those who are criticized the most. Rosenshine (1971) found that even if teachers inform students that their work is incorrect, this is positively correlated with academic improvement! Praise is not only saying a word or two to a student about achievement, but it is also owning congruent body language to support those positive statements. For example, it is not effective to say, "Good job on your exam" without a smile or other emphasis. Also, the overuse of praise or the use of non-contingent praise are easily detected and not appreciated by students.

8. Reasons for Praise--behaviorists tell us that praise needs to be contingent on the appropriate behavior(s) we are trying to reinforce. Instead of just offering a vague comment to a student like "Good", it is much more affective/effective to specify the contingent behavior--"I am well-pleased with the quiet way you have worked for the last fifteen minutes!" In the same manner, it is very important to realize that praise in the form of only

"As" (for grades) without written feedback does not maintain motivation. If students continually expect As--because they haven't been informed as to how to improve themselves--they will eventually kick back and expect more As with less work. I've had students come into my office and say, "Dr. R. I'm an A student. Why have I received a B on this assignment?" I then proceed to review the feedback on the back page of the assignment. I highlight ways that the student may improve. Many students are not used to this kind of interaction; their response initially is "Oh." Lev Vygotsky talks about the zone of proximal development. It is imperative to student engagement in learning and therefore, to student success that we teach students at the level at which they are functioning cognitively, but also to challenge them, with help one level above that level at which they are able to work themselves. Offering feedback as a challenge is teaching to the zone of proximal development.

9.   Listening--Students in many classrooms are expected to spend the majority of the time listening to the teachers. Slavin tells us that it is **interaction** between teacher and student, between student and student that enhances achievement. Do teachers really listen to students? Do students really listen to other students? The literature shows that teachers listen to low achieving students less than they listen to high achieving students. A sign of good listening--active listening--is associated with eye contact and a rephrasing of what the student has said. The coined, "I hear you saying that...", although seemingly superficial, is a definite technique used to develop good listening skills.   In a "Comparison of Communication Activities", Adler and Towne show that although listening is learned first, and used the most, it is taught the least in classrooms.[6]   There are many, many resources for teachers to use to teach active listening skills among students. These are skills, by the way, which need to be at least reviewed before any cooperative learning groups may be productive. Students' awareness of teachers listening to them is reflected in positive feelings for the teachers by the students. These positive feelings are the framework of an affective relationship.

10. Accepting Feelings--an important component of engagement in learning is the acceptance of feelings. It is crucial for the teacher not only to accept his/her feelings, but it is also important for the teacher to accept students' feelings. A very common segment of any video regarding classroom management will comment on the importance for the teacher to allow

students to vent their feelings about whatever has riled them before attempting to settle into the work of the day. If students' energies are vested on emotional issues, there is not much energy left for homework. If a teacher dismisses an emotional climate and moves directly into a presentation of new information,

this new information stands a good chance of being lost. A simple example of the need to deal with students' feelings is the following: I taught reading right after lunch. Many of my seventh graders stormed into the classroom upset about events over the noon hour--especially boy-girl interactions on the playground. If I had continuously overlooked these feelings of the students and continued to teach, I'd find myself reteaching a great deal of information. Instead on many occasions, I allowed the students to vent, air their feelings. To my surprise, many times I was able to use the discussion as a transition into the lesson for the day!

Part of the problem with the acceptance of feelings, is that many of us, students and teachers alike, are not able to identify feelings. Have you ever listened to a seventh grader respond to the question, "How are you today?" You may hear, "O.K.", "Huh?" and various other grunts. One day in my classroom I used a "feelings chart". I explained to the students that over 400 different English words have been identified to name emotions. I asked them to choose a facial expression on the chart that seemed to reflect their feelings and to respond to the question, "How are you today?" with a feeling word. Many were quite surprised to learn that the original "O.K." was replaced by "depressed", "angry", "anxious", etc. Students (and teachers) also need to understand that negative emotions are normal. Role-playing offers excellent situations in which students can learn to cope with their emotions.

The third strand of the TESA interaction model revolves around PERSONAL REGARD as a strategy of affective teaching:

11. Proximity--Proximity refers to nearness/closeness. It is interesting to me that teachers who especially seem to have problems with classroom management are those teachers who are planted in one spot in the front of the classroom--like the teacher in my study who, within a 45 minute period, took only one step to the right of her podium (at the front of the room) and one step back. Why is it difficult for some teachers to understand that students really want to perceive them as human? Why can't some teachers drop their security blankets and actually venture down an aisle or two of students? This movement is an incredibly simple strategy for classroom

management. As I move around my students, up and down the aisles during the first few weeks of classes, I tell the students that just as they get "up tight" as I approach them, that this is a really scary thing for me to do. I often add, "You're a tough audience!" which relieves some of the anxiety in the room. Proximity is a means of showing students that you're interested in them and in what they're doing. It is also a tool for classroom management.

12. Courtesy--In the preface of this book, I opened with my experience of surprise that a textbook would included "how to"s for teachers in regard to fairness in treatment of all students. For me, this is understood--just as is courtesy . As long ago as 1970, *Crisis in the Classroom* by Silberman stated, "We decry...the lack of civility among the young, particularly the young demonstrators--but one seeks in vain for civility in the classroom. What one observes instead is the sheer rudeness with which most teachers speak to children as a matter of course. They don't say 'please', they don't say 'thank you', they simply give orders with no explanation. If we adults do not respect the youngsters, how can we expect them to respect each other?[7]

I guess we need to teach courtesy. Who would have thought that would be necessary? One of my daughters recently voiced a concern that her teacher never said thank you to the students. At a parent conference I asked the teacher if that was the case. She said it was, that she didn't feel she had to thank students for doing something that was their responsibility to complete in the first place! My first thought to her response was, "Boy!". Even though it's my responsibility to deal with problems among students and faculty--a job that's not so pleasant at times--I still like to be thanked every once in a while for the effort! The Golden Rule proposes that we treat our students as we like to be treated. If a teacher is courteous, a student perceives the courtesy as respect--a very important building block for an affective relationship.

13. Personal Interest and Compliments--If students are given the opportunity to share their personal experiences, they will become more willing to do so. Students love to listen to the life experiences of others, even of the teacher. My son tells me on a regular basis how his teacher takes a break every once in a while to allow for story-telling. Classes that are highly interactive, including the sharing of life experiences of not only the students but of the teacher, as well, seem to be the favorite classes of my children. Praise of learning performance may also be incorporated when

students' stories are related to the learning tasks for the day. A teacher who shows personal interest in his/her students will ask questions or compliment students.

14. Touching--Touch is certainly a controversial topic, especially in my Ed. Psych. sections. I show a video about developmentally appropriate programming in which a first grade male teacher allows female students to sit in his lap when the class comes together in a sharing circle. The debate begins in my classroom. I have had prospective teachers tell me that they will never touch children, and that if the situation occurred simultaneously as it happens in the video, that they would simply tell the students to get out of their laps! The ensuing discussion focuses on the child's self-esteem and feelings. I only ask my students to rethink their positions. I validate their feelings of discomfort, and I tell them that they have to be comfortable in order to teach effectively, but they also need to take into consideration the impact of their behaviors on the children/students. We discuss the "procedures for touch" that are outlined in some districts' handbooks. We also share personal experiences of touch in the classroom. Touch, for many students, yields a feeling of acceptance, belongingness.

15. Desisting--Desisting is doing something to stop a misbehavior; desisting usually reflects effective classroom management. Hostile desisting is noneffective. Rosenshine (1971) found that "hostile, threatening desists relate to lack of growth in reading, whereas non-threatening desists relate to reading achievement."[8] Desisting may be done in many ways. The simplest way is to incorporate non-verbal behavior--the "look." Desisting in a calm and courteous manner spares the misbehaving student a put-down and serves as an example for the rest of the class. The teacher who is an effective classroom manager is perceived by students as one who values education and one who respects students.

Hopefully, in reading through this list of tried and tested affective strategies, you will be able to identify many that you are now incorporating into your own classroom. Again, these interactions are supported by a wealth of educational literature; their ties to academic growth are noted in the literature. We can all instruct affectively, and this affective instruction is not difficult to accomplish. A simple smile and a greeting at the classroom door are the beginning to the development of rapport with a student. These **TESA** strategies will enhance your effectiveness as a teacher.

Notes

1. Gallos in "On the Art of Teaching Management," 446.
2. Phi Delta Kappa, TESA Manual, 1980.
3. Op cit., A-23.
4. Op cit., D-1.
5. Op cit., D-38-39.
6. Adler and Towne, *Looking Out, Looking In*, 282.
7. Silberman in *Crisis in the Classroom*.
8. Rosenshine in *Teaching Behaviors and Student Achievement*.

References

Adler, R. and N. Towne (1996). *Looking Out, Looking In*. Texas: Harcourt Brace.
Gallos, J. "On the Art of Teaching Management," Journal of Management
Education, 21, 4.
Phi Delta Kappa. *Teacher Expectations and Student Achievement (TESA)*.
        Indiana: Phi Delta Kappa (P.O. Box 789, Bloomington, IN, 47402).
Rosenshine, Barak (1971). *Teaching Behaviors and Student Achievement*.
        London: National Foundation for Educational Research in England and
        Wales.
Silberman, C. (1971). *Crisis in the Classroom: The Remaking of American
        Education*. New York: Random House.
Slavin, R. (2000). *Educational Psychology*. Massachusetts: Allyn and Bacon.

CHAPTER 3--AFFECTIVE EDUCATIONAL SETTINGS

My first three children were delivered by the obstetrician who delivered me. Actually, he isn't ancient; he always told me that he just graduated from medical school at a young age! Because this doctor was schooled in "the old way", I never had a choice as to whether I could deliver in a birthing room, a more updated option. My doctor always said that if something should happen, he needed to have the staff and the equipment readily available for any emergency. He didn't have time to "monkey around" transporting me to the surgical area.

After my obstetrician's retirement, I had a fourth child. With a new doctor, I was given the chance to deliver in a birthing room. I imagine that I could write a chapter or two on the differences in these two experiences. My fourth child--by far, the largest at 11 pounds 2 ½ ounces!--was the most easily delivered. My comfort level in the birthing room, I'm sure, played an important role in the ease of delivery.

Birthing rooms were designed to facilitate deliveries by offering to the mothers and their husbands an atmosphere of attractiveness, warmth, and peacefulness. They are meant to replace the cold, noisy, sterile atmosphere of the regular surgical room. The "homeyness" of the birthing room is definitely a positive factor that sells this option for expectant moms.

Affective educational settings are those that are able to "sell" learning. How many times have we, as students, sat in undecorated, poorly lit, terribly painted, classrooms where all the desks are in neat rows? What types of things do you remember about your learning in these classrooms? Was it your best year in school? Your worst? Did you learn a lot? Or were you distracted out of boredom? I think you are able to predict the descriptions of affective settings that lie ahead in this chapter!

In a survey of my students several years ago, I collected some interesting responses when I asked students how the facility--the building, itself--could be improved. Here are some student responses:

> *If colors in classrooms were brighter the students and
> teachers would be brighter.

> *I think the classrooms would be better if they were

decorated. Interesting prints could be put on the walls. Most of the classrooms are decorated with only a clock. That is so boring! It's hard to learn in a room that bores a person to death.

*Please have classrooms with windows. Also, classrooms should not be over-crowded. You'd be surprised how a classroom can influence one's state of mind.

*Some of the classrooms are so gloomy. Add some pictures.

*The classrooms are dirty and dusty. The rooms are dull; a little color would help.

*Does anyone check the lighting in these rooms? I think if someone would count, they would come up with the same number of burned out bulbs as I did--six out of fifteen.

I need to update these responses, since the school has been in a constant state of reconstruction and decoration over the last several years. Students and faculty notice and appreciate the brightly colored walls and the decorations, to name a few improvements.

We need to continuously acquire feedback from those we are charged to instruct. This risky questioning of students is an affective strategy. We are seeking clarification of their needs, descriptions of "homeyness" that can make learning more appealing.

When I was a middle school teacher, I continuously was in trouble with the maintenance staff. The janitors "turned me in to the principal" because, as they put it, "[I] had so much junk in my room!" I remember the project on primitive cultures that I did with sixth graders. The students had to create clothing without any use of technology. They could opt to paint a picture, a cave drawing, without using brushes, etc. So as the groups of students began to collect their materials in nature, they brought them into the classroom where they could continue their work in their free times. We had rocks, dried flowers, branches, leaves, and mud on the tables. The students' hands-on projects were a hit! They begged to do more. However, the janitor refused to move everything around on a daily basis in order to clean. He also complained about the solar system mobiles that always seemed to hit him in the head when he attempted to clean the floor. The cereal boxes that had been affixed to the reading corner walls were not a favorite of the janitor, either! I was determined that the maintenance staff would not dictate the hands-on activities that my students were craving. So, that year I cut a deal with the staff. If they would only continue to clean my blackboards and empty my wastebaskets, I would clean the floor every night as long as I knew where the broom was kept.

When I was invited back to those sixth graders' graduation ceremony, it was about those messy projects that they enjoyed reminiscing. We shared many laughs about how I had been "turned in" to the principal for having so much "junque" (my spelling!) in the classroom.

There are many aspects of an affective educational setting. Most of these aspects are quite "mechanical" in nature; a simple rearrangement of students desks is an affective teaching strategy. I don't expect instructors to replace desks with Stratoloungers and to serve soft drinks and chips during class, but I would like to see some flexibility in the way that rooms are arranged and decorated. I always told my Ed. Psych. students that I could choose an affective teacher for my children, especially in the elementary schools, without ever meeting the teacher. I would simply walk down the hallway of a school and sneak a peak at the classrooms. Were the children all seated in rows and ABSOLUTELY quiet? Or was there a sense of organized chaos within the classroom, a result of students busily working with their friends? Were walls decorated with CHILDREN'S work? Or was the teacher proclaiming to be too busy in to have decorated the walls with student work?

An affective teacher considers all of the following aspects of classroom (dis)order in creating an affective educational setting:

PERSONAL GREETINGS--affective teachers will greet their students at the door. They will have already prepped for class, so they are able to offer genuine concern and interest as the students enter the classroom. For instructors of older students, who may change from class to class, this means that the instructor greets students each time the roster changes. One of my college students was a little baffled to see me outside of the classroom door during the first week of class. He asked me if the class was writing an instructor evaluation. I was unclear as to what he was asking, so I pressed further. He explained that instructors only stand outside of the classroom when it was time for the students to complete their course evaluations. He had thought that it was a little early in the course for an evaluation. I asked if he had ever had a professor greet him at the door, for that was my reason in standing outside of the classroom. He responded, "Never. I've been here two years. Never!"

SEATING ARRANGEMENTS--Teachers truly need to be flexible when it comes to the seating arrangements of their students. Many instructors tell students that they **MUST** seat students alphabetically or that the students **MUST** stay in the same seats all year because school policy "says so!" The rationale behind the school policy is that should a substitute teacher come into the room, the seating chart is there to help eliminate disciplinary problems. If this is your school's policy, talk to the principal or to the superintendent. If you were to ask students where they wanted to sit, inevitably they'd answer, "By [their] friends". So why not allow them to sit "by their friends"? You might ask, "Well, am I not creating just the atmosphere for them to talk?" My response is "Yes, and so what?" Vygotsky talks about the importance of peers sharing discussion for the purpose of future problem-solving through private speech. Affective teachers, who have developed a positive rapport with their students, are able to simply tell students when they can talk with their friends and when they shouldn't. Students will, for the most part, respect the wishes of the teacher. They are especially thankful that they don't have to sit alphabetically; they are willing to respect the classroom rules of order.

In a traditional classroom seating arrangement--four or five rows of five or six students--the teacher is known to interact primarily with those students who sit in the "**T**" formation; that is, the teacher will call most frequently on the students who sit right down the middle row and those students who sit across the top row. I like to share this information with my students early in the semester, because then if they don't want to participate in a particular class, they might choose one of the outlying seats! When they report to me that the strategy didn't work, I respond, "Ha! You have a truly affective teacher!" (Of course, affectiveness is not identified on the basis of only one teaching strategy!)

If the teacher insists on a classroom with "rows", it is imperative for her or him to interact with every student in the classroom, no matter where that student is sitting. (More is said about this interaction in Chapter 2).

The classroom arrangement that I have found to be most well-liked by the students is that of pods of three, four, or five. This is a very necessary arrangement for cooperative learning, but it is also a more comfortable, friendly arrangement than the conventional rows. Although it is necessary to assign students to cooperative learning groups, the pods help to create a comfortable setting for the students. Books and backpacks can be tucked under desks to make this very "do-able"; the congestion caused by books and backpacks is a common excuse offered by teachers for avoiding such a seating arrangement.

THE WALLS--Students (and faculty) need to have something to look at in classrooms other than the clock at the front of the room. Posters are colorful messages for students of all ages. Student work is also a must! Students of all ages love to see their work on the bulletin boards and walls. To seek student permission before hanging work is a sign of respect between teacher and students. Several examples come to mind from my teaching career as I write this...

I shared a room once with another teacher who thought it would be a good idea to put students' work in the hallway outside of our classroom door. When I returned to the classroom one afternoon I noticed maps and essays on the wall. Upon closer inspection, I discovered that all of the papers had been graded, and not one of them had a grade higher than a "C-"! I asked my colleague why she would put next-to-failing student work on the wall for 400+ peers to view. Her response was, "I thought it was a good way to get the students to do better work." I politely asked her to remove those papers from OUR classroom wall. When she refused, I asked the principal to intervene. He did. My relationship with the teacher needed fixing, but I needed to prevent the taunting that the students were sure to receive from their peers. It seems we can all learn a lot from others' mistakes.

On a more positive note...for a college Ed. Psych. class, I had my students "create a picture of an effective/affective teacher". That was all I told them, other than to be creative. Some of their ideas were lovely. I had poetry to read, surprise boxes in which to discover secrets of teaching, posters, collages, and so on. With students' permission, I made a grand display of work in the hallway outside of my office. I wish I had recorded the number of positive comments the students and I received because their work was on display. This truly was a verification for me that students of ALL ages love to see their work on display.

Fresh paint and student murals are also ways of making the classroom more comfortable. I remember a grade school year where we were allowed during every free period to work on the mural we had begun in conjunction with our unit in on Egypt. That was one of my most favorite projects in grade school; perhaps, the pride of ownership had something to do with that.

WINDOWS--I taught for three years in a school in which only two classrooms had windows; I was never lucky enough to acquire one of those classrooms. I found myself going outside at the lunch hour, even in the wintertime. I could never understand why schools were designed without windows in every classroom. Perhaps, in this particular case, the lack of windows bolstered the myth that middle schools are simply warehouses for raging adolescents! Many classrooms without windows have murals of windows and scenes to enhance the atmosphere. When our school was remodeled--when permanent walls replaced fiberboard dividers from the "open classroom era", windows were also added. Both students and teachers become more alive in a more spacious, brighter setting.

HALLWAYS–As a fourth grade teacher, I was aware of an all-school problem–that of students racing through the halls and around corners. The proximity of teachers was effective, but it was not always possible for enough teachers to patrol the halls during passing periods, especially. I took on the problem as a class project. With the principal's approval and a small budget, my students and I transformed our hallway into a highway. We included road signs and especially, "no passing" yellow lines. The students thought the idea was great! They overemphasized their stops at stop signs. They reminded their peers to "stay to the right." Soon other school hallways were transformed, as well. The relevancy, practicality of the activity seemed to ensure its success.

OTHER CLASSROOM FEATURES--I wrote before, tongue-in-cheek, about the Stratalounger in the classroom. I would venture a guess, however, that if students were asked to name a favorite teacher, or a class in which they felt they retained the most amount of information, it would be the teacher who allowed comfortable seating arrangements or the class in which the big easy chair had been recycled. Private areas for independent work are oftentimes inclusive of oversized stuffed chairs or even bathtubs! Have you ever seen a bathtub in a classroom? Students vie for the opportunity to "lounge" in the tub during silent reading period. This idea, of course, mostly pertains to elementary and middle school classrooms, but instructors of undergraduate students can certainly follow the lead presented by teachers of younger students. Affective college instructors, if not able to provide super-comfortable seating for their students, are at least able to allow students to break midst a long, tedious presentation. The break, that is usually shared with friends, is most appreciated by the students. Also, that oversized stuffed chair that won't work too well in the college classroom might be located in the instructor's office and offered to the student when he or she visits!

There is a great deal to be said about the negative reinforcers in the classroom, which when removed from the situation, increase student involvement and participation. Some of these negative reinforcers are loud noise--usually from the hallway or from adjacent rooms, extreme heat--usually from improperly functioning radiators, especially in older buildings, poor lighting--highly conducive to "nap time" among college students, and extreme cold--in many cases, this is a complaint of students who aren't used to air conditioning. Learning theory tells us that performance will increase if these negative reinforcers are eliminated from the setting. In many cases, their elimination simply requires a call to the maintenance staff.

I taught an Ed. Psych. class one winter term in a small, closed room in the basement. We met together for three weeks--all day Monday and Tuesday and for a half day on Thursday. There were only twelve students in the class, but by the time we entered our third hour together, the air seemed stifling. In addition, because the blackboards were not cleaned on a regular basis, the accumulation of chalk dust caused one student, in particular, to sneeze frequently. The situation was corrected simply by requesting a daily cleaning of the blackboards, by opening one of the adjacent classroom's doors, and by allowing a few more frequent breaks during the day.

It is not difficult to create an affective educational setting. To bring a classroom alive can be accomplished by bringing living things into the room. Flowers or plants on a teacher's desk or on a table are a nice addition to any classroom. Frogs, toads, salamanders, bunnies, and other "pets" are also enjoyed by most students. One of my daughters has vivid memories--and a wealth of knowledge--from her high school biology class. She often tells the story about the big, white bird that landed on her shoulder during class and left a few droppings on her t-shirt. This was one of her most memorable classes in school.

Most of the already mentioned ideas deal with the physical aspect of the learning setting--desks, lighting, heat, etc. There are many other factors that generate affectiveness; these factors involve the personality or demeanor of the classroom teacher. Chapter 1 of this book summarizes the characteristics of teachers who have been identified as affective. The affective teacher personalizes the learning experience. She focuses on students' needs and presents information in such a way that it is tied to these individual needs. The affective teacher stimulates students. He concerns himself with guaranteeing a positive student attitude toward learning. The affective teacher motivates students. He listens, attends, bans put-downs, gets involved, and displays positive regard for others.

I traditionally set the groundwork for a debate in my Ed. Psych. classroom regarding the question, "Is it possible to teach one to be a good, effective/affective teacher, or does one need that special built-in 'something' in order to be a master teacher?" The premise of the debate, of course, is that prospective teachers have the desire to be effective. We have spent an entire 75 minute class period debating this issue. Ultimately, the consensus is, "Yes, we are, indeed, capable of teaching teachers to become affective." I am always pleased with the consensus, and I state my pleasure by defining the purpose of an Ed. Psych. class. The students have validated my employment as an Ed. Psych. instructor.

Of all of the affective qualities that are mentioned in Chapter 1, it is probably most important to reiterate the importance of a teacher's *unconditional positive regard* for students. Carl Rogers is given the credit for this concept. It refers to one's acknowledgment and acceptance of an individual simply because this individual exists; there are no strings attached to the regard. For teachers, unconditional positive regard means that **ALL** students are respected, no matter the background, family income, culture, ethnicity, or gender. The words, "writing off a student" are not in an affective teacher's vocabulary. The affective teacher does not regard a student more positively because of higher scores on tests or because of the student's lingering after class to talk with the instructor. This regard paves the way for equal treatment of **ALL** students. If you have not yet read the editorial preface of this book, please do so now. The question in the example given in the first paragraph of the preface may seem, at this time, most inappropriate. For a student, the prospective teacher, to even ask whether he needs to respect all students, makes one wonder how this notion even developed!

I'd like to close this chapter with some more of the comments that I collected from undergraduate students when they were asked if they had any suggestions for instructors. You will notice that many of these comments are requests for an affective approach to teaching--affective teachers in an affective setting:

> *Smile more.
> *Help students to accept that they have biases, help them
>   to identify them and to become more aware of them.
> *Have a sense of humor. (Some students tell me that as
>   prospective teachers they are worried about a lack of a
>   sense of humor. We discuss, that if this is the case, there
>   are so many ways to integrate humor into the classroom.
>   Students usually always think of showing a funny movie
>   or video to their students.)

*I have noticed for a long time that this campus has
favoritism from some professors.
*Say, "Hello" to us, even in the hallways.
*Be a little more approachable. Be available during office
hours and after class.
*Treat each person as an individual. If a student tells you
something about his/her life situation, listen and be
understanding. Don't assume that everyone is the same.

It needs to be stated at this point in this discourse, especially for the
naysayers, that the primary focus in education is **NOT** the comfort level of
the students. It is, however, highly reflective of the respect that the teacher
holds for students, an element of effective/affective teaching that is
highlighted in the educational literature.

Part II--How Do We Emphasize the Affective Domain in Teaching?

The first part of this book has dealt with general information about the affective domain and more specific information regarding the integration of affective strategies within our instructional plans. This second part of the book will attempt to tie everything together. Chapter 4 focuses on the symbiotic relationship between the affective and cognitive domains. Not once does the author of this book attempt to deflect the importance of the cognitive domain. Rather, I strive to emphasize the importance of both domains. It seems that many a radio talk show host will choose to dichotomize, or split the cognitive and affective domains in order to minimize the importance of the affective domain and even make light of any affective focus in education: "Why is it so important for students to FEEL good? How can FEELING good help them to learn? Isn't it about time that students face reality and experience that which does not FEEL good? Isn't this when learning actually occurs?"

The affective domain **DOES NOT JUST FOCUS ON FEELING GOOD.** Rather, the good feeling is a result of positive teacher-student interactions. Teachers who address students' needs, teachers who present relevant, up-to-date, and practical information are, in essence, creating a positive climate for learning. Students have a road map telling them where they are going or where they may go with new information. School and learning are given new meaning. A value is placed on education. When students clearly see the relevancy of instruction, they are motivated to learn more. Motivation breeds success. Success affords a good feeling or a heightened self-esteem. Nowhere in this manuscript does the good feeling outweigh the success of the learner. In fact, one cannot tease the two apart! This symbiotic relationship is discussed in Chapter 4.

A "how-to" manual is not complete without an assessment tool. Chapter 5 offers many questions for the reader, which when answered in the affirmative, point to a particular level of teacher affectiveness. Are we affective and effective teachers? We probably are by the fact that we are incorporating many affective strategies in our presentations. Is there room for improvement? **ALWAYS!**

Chapter 5 also provides us with suggestions regarding affective interactions with students. Hopefully, these reminders will be helpful to the individual or to an entire staff within a school. Many of the suggestions have many years of educational research. **Why not listen to the students?**

CHAPTER 4--THE SYMBIOTIC RELATIONSHIP BETWEEN THE COGNITIVE AND AFFECTIVE DOMAINS

Throughout each of these chapters, there is a definite emphasis on the affective domain. This emphasis, in no way, minimizes the importance of the cognitive domain. **Symbiosis** is from the Greek **sumbiosis** meaning "living together". This close association of the two domains is complementary. The integration of the cognitive and affective elements of learning have been termed "confluent education" or "humanistic education".[1]

In the 1970s, the Ford-Esalen Project (funded by the Ford Foundation) was developed through the Esalen Institute of California. It focused on problems in education and attempted to resolve these problems by integrating the cognitive and the affective domains. "Affective" was defined by the Esalen Institute as "the feeling or emotional aspect of learning and experience." Traditional education seemed, to the developers of the Esalen Project, focused on the cognitive only. It was thought, however, to be realistic to believe that whenever one learned intellectually, that there was an inseparable accompanying emotion; this affective dimension connoted a personal relevance. "The relationship between intellect and affect is indestructibly symbiotic."[2]

In an attempt, then, to "renew the whole man" within the educational process, the Esalen Project's team set out to show that the integration of both domains, the cognitive and the affective, benefits both domains:

> Educators, by compressing and organizing knowledge in all areas of the curriculum have created what Paul Tillich has called the 'fatal pedagogical error'--to throw answers like stones at the heads of those who have not yet asked the questions. Not only has this reinforced and compounded the pathological condition of unfeeling, but it has also had a significant negative effect on cognitive learning, itself.[3]

Teacher instruction may reflect the symbiotic relationship between the cognitive and the affective domains. Good and Brophy (1977) write of affective development as similar to cognitive development. Concrete experiences are influenced by feedback from others. These experiences frame an individual's concept of self. Her/His view or perception of what s/he can or cannot do is formed. "Affective behaviors develop when appropriate learning experiences are provided for students much the same as cognitive behavior develops from appropriate learning experiences". Students and teachers are able to learn caring or affective behavior.[4]

Bloom, Krathwohl, and Masia (1956) divided educational objectives into the psychomotor, cognitive and affective domains; a taxonomy for each domain was developed. An overlap of goals for the two domains is evident when one compares the taxonomy of the affective domain to Bloom's taxonomy of the cognitive domain.

The taxonomy of educational objectives pertinent to the affective domain, or the domain of emotional response according to Bloom (1964), is comprised of the following objectives:

1. Receiving--attending to something in the environment
2. Responding--new behavior is a result of an experience
3. Valuing--a decision is made to become involved in or committed to a particular activity
4. Organization--a prioritization of a new value becomes an important part of one's set of values, and
5. Characterization by value--behavior is displayed that is consistent with a new value

This taxonomy of the affective domain frames inner growth once "a person grows aware of, and then adopts attitudes, principles, codes, and sanctions that support value judgments and guide behavior".[5]

To examine these individual objectives is an important component of affective teaching. The "receiving" objective is crucial to student engagement. It is the responsibility of the instructor to SNATCH the attention of the student. This can be done in many ways--through motions, change in position, unusual clothing (dressing in character), inflection of voice, and relevant instruction, to name a few. The instructor must gain the attention of the student in order for the student to "receive" information. The Atkinson-Shiffrin (1968) model of information processing states that one must pay attention to information if s/he wants to retain it.

There can be many responses to stimuli in the environment. Responses may be positive or negative, genuine or insincere. Affective teachers are able to reinforce appropriate responses effectively. The teacher who listens, who affirms or corrects, who accepts students' feelings and praises is one who influences the strength of the response.

In the "valuing" stage, the learner ascribes value to a particular stimulus. There may be something intriguing about a stimulus that warrants further investigation. It is the affective instructor who certainly encourages students to explore their environments. Hands-on activities and visual presentations hold the interests of students. The Level of Processing Theory (Craik & Lockhart, 1972) states that the more one attends to details, the more likely one is to remember information about an object. An affective teacher displays an object, names its parts, and identifies its use. The object may be handled, listened to, smelled and tasted by students. This object, subjected to different levels of processing, will most likely be recalled easily by the students. Valuation of the object is encouraged; interaction with the object occurs.

Through the "organization" phase, one integrates a valued stimulus (from the previous stage) into his behavioral repertoire. An affective teacher who role models social skills for her students may soon observe the students enacting those skills in their attempts to befriend a peer. Personal responses to situational dilemmas may afford students the opportunity to test competing values.

The final, or "characterization by value" stage, finds one thinking, behaving, and feeling a particular way because of a value that has become a part of one's (value) system, personality. One who values volunteerism, will be seen volunteering and focusing on altruistic efforts. It is important to note the overlap of the two domains in the previous two stages. Through synthesis and evaluation--educational objectives of the cognitive domain-- one is able to more clearly "organize", or integrate a valued stimulus. This integration, in turn, leads to "characterization".

The overlap of the cognitive and affective domains introduced, it is important to present the cognitive objectives in their entirety. Bloom's taxonomy of educational objectives of the cognitive domain are knowledge, comprehension, application, analysis, synthesis, and evaluation. No valuation, interest, attitude nor feeling is ascribed to any of the first five objectives of human learning. A student, through rote memory, for example, may learn material very well without ever affixing a value to it; it may have been learned simply because it was assigned. It is the "evaluation" objective that is often confused with the "organization" phase of the affective domain. However, although a value may frame, "inform an evaluation process, the evaluation behavior is, itself, discrete. An example would be the determination on the part of a nurse to increase the dosage of a medication for a patient solely on the basis of the patient's condition."[6]

Dressel (1988) and Piaget[7] write of the importance of recognizing the symbiotic relationship between the affective and the cognitive means of knowing. Dressel states that this recognition "better enables children to think critically and to care deeply".[8] According to Piaget, both the cognitive and affective systems are closely interrelated. Coining the term "affective schema", Piaget refers to experiences of affects that regulate action: "affectivity regulates the energetic aspect of action, of which intelligence provides the structure. Affective life, similar to intellectual life, is continuous adaptation, and both of these adaptations are not only parallel but interdependent, since sentiments express the interests and values of actions of which intelligence constitutes the structure".[9]

Elbaz (1992) also mentions the importance of broadening the concentration on cognitive aspects to include the moral dimension. Elbaz states that the concrete knowledge of children underlying hopefulness[10] points to moral implications of teachers' thinking: "In their attentiveness, teachers acknowledge that certainty is unavailable but that they are morally bound to act anyhow according to their best understanding of children's interests."[11]

Sonnier (1982) intertwines the cognitive and affective domains in her discussions of holistic education; in order to teach the **whole** person, one must focus on both domains. Sonnier says that too often the affective learning and cognitive achievement are considered mutually exclusive results. Her theory, at times criticized as being over-simplified, states that the affective domain is a function of the right hemispheric processes, and the cognitive domain is one of the left hemispheric processes. Affectivity and left brain activities are complementary in learning. Nevertheless, the researcher's focus on the **symbiotic** relationship between the two domains is echoed in the literature, particularly in that of humanistic education. Sonnier continues, those who are driven within the classroom to teach "reach students through their heads. Those who attempt to teach the whole person and concentrate on the learning act, reach students' heads through their hearts".[12]

Sonnier emphasizes that educators must be committed to teaching all students, students of great diversity. "The dignity and integrity of different individuals MUST be held in sacred trust by all teachers. In everyday terms, each individual MUST be made to feel good about himself". To understand diversity among students is to reach, or engage, many more students. To approach diversity, one needs to employ a holistic strategy. Sonnier believes every teacher has the ability to teach holistically, or to teach to students' needs. Affective learning is not attained at the sacrifice of cognitive learning, for affective learning is acquired through a reduction of feelings of despair, perhaps, surrounding individual differences. Sonnier suggests that student-centered activities or those that are holistically oriented should be used to promote unity, healing, and self-concept.

Gazda also speaks of a holistic approach to learning:

> If teachers are facilitators of learning, they must start where the student is psychologically. He or she is where his or her feelings are. Feelings are the energy source. When students feel negative about their school work, energy is absent or misdirected. Energy is present when teachers relate subject matter in ways which arouse positive feelings. Positive feelings are most likely to occur when students feel good about themselves.[13]

Student-centered activities, as suggested by Sonnier, are those kinds of affective experiences Bayer (1986) described as affecting self-concept. Bayer found self-concept to be relatively stable over time, changing only according to certain experiences like family structure and teachers' personal views of students' abilities. Bayer cited Wylie's research (1969-1971) as evidence of the fact that there is definitely a relationship between self-concept and achievement. Bayer stated that it was, therefore, important to pursue the study between teacher behavior and student outcomes, or the relationship between personal interaction and achievement. In so doing, Bayer found that psychological growth occurred only through personally meaningful experiences. Bayer concluded that affective experiences boost self-esteem which, in turn, impact on achievement. In a study by Prawat in 1985, almost half of the sample of ninety teachers identified a focus on the affective domain as its most important goal. "Teachers were most concerned with fostering interpersonal adjustment as well as aspects of intrapersonal adjustment, such as self-concept".[14] Affective strategies/programming were also identified as an important goal for teachers in regard to enhancement of student engagement in learning.

This presentation, thus far, is quite "heady" for the average reader. What is lacking in regard to the element that will aid the reader in remembering the information is the affective dimension. Had I included story after story and personal comments within the presentation, I may have succeeded in assisting your memory. However, as written, you probably now have to go back through the last five pages to highlight the main points in order to apply them to your teaching. This is why Educational

Psychology texts are so interesting. A great deal of learning theory is presented and then, the voices of students and teachers are included to complement/reinforce the "heady" presentations. I could continue *ad nauseum* with a review of the literature pertaining to the symbiotic relationship between the cognitive and affective domains. Suffice it to say, that this topic has been reviewed by educators for over forty years.

Effective teaching is often measured by the amount of information that students learn; one question on the teacher evaluation form that students are asked to complete at Concordia University is, "How much did you learn in this course?" (Students answer using a Likert scale with "5"= "Much" and "1"="Little".) Just as I cannot be effective in my transmission of knowledge through mere written presentation of a knowledge base, so is it with the classroom instructor who may not be able to impart his or her knowledge without integrating affective strategies. Learning in the cognitive domain is definitely influenced by the affective domain. Those Educational Psychology texts are replete with suggestions as to how to meet students' individual needs. Constructivist theory is defined and learning through discovery is explained. Effective lecturing is also identified. So many instructors, by the way, tune out "affectiveness" because they perceive it as threatening their lecture style. There are gadzillions of affective lecturers in the world, but they just don't lecture, they incorporate affective strategies in their presentations. By simply "coming up for air" and stopping to ask a few questions of the students might be considered an affective strategy. The instructor is, then, focused on the needs of the students--their comprehension of the material that was presented through direct instruction. I recall one student comment regarding suggestions as to how instructors could become more affective in the classroom: "I often find that most instructors are wrapped up in presenting information. They become less of a teacher and more of a presenter-of-information. I realize that at the college level, we no longer call professors "teachers", however, has their role changed? I believe instructors need to remember they are teachers. I can pick up my text and read it and go to the library for supplemental information, but it is the teacher who should help me understand it. The teacher needs to empower the student to say, 'Yes, I understand!' In **teaching only**, there is learning".

I highlighted the "teaching only" because I think the implication is clear that this student, and the majority of students in general, appreciate and gain from the overlap of the cognitive and affective domains. The survey that was used to collect student responses as the aforementioned, includes the definition of an "affective teacher" as one "who interacts often with students, one who has friendly classrooms, and one who holds high expectations of students (Cobb, 1992). An affective teacher is also identified as kind, friendly, cheerful, patient, helpful, fair, in possession of a sense of humor, and able to understand students' problems. An affective teacher maintains order in the classroom, is not sarcastic, and provides for the needs of individual pupils (Gazda, 1977). In short, an affective teacher is approachable, easy to relate to, caring, perceptive, and tolerant." These characteristics can be taught. I always offer the question to my students, "Is it possible to teach teachers affective qualities, or are they innate?" We usually debate this for about fifteen minutes after which I let the students know that it's a good thing that we **are** able to teach affectiveness as this ability secures my job as an educational psychologist!

So...if the literature says that there is a strong relationship, symbiotic, in fact, between the cognitive and affective domains, and students echo the desire for their instructors to be affective, why do we have so many who dismiss the affective domain as the least important domain of learning? A great factor is fear, fear of change. If one does change teaching strategies and finds success in affectiveness, it might place blame on the teacher for not changing sooner. Who is in focus here? The teacher or the student? I've been regarded as an idealist, and perhaps, this is one of my idealist statements, but..."Why wouldn't all teachers strive to become more affective?" By incorporating small bits of this chapter and others of the book, through practice and feedback, many can develop affective teaching strategies on their own. Did you know that students appreciate being greeted at the classroom door? They actually want teachers to get to know them and to ask, "How are things going?" These are not difficult things for an instructor to do. And...this is the beginning of affectiveness in the classroom.

Once simple affective strategies are incorporated into the school day, teachers can move on to "bigger and better things." A very important element of affective teaching--integrating the cognitive and affective domains--is affective programming. Since the final chapter of this book includes many more suggestions of affective teaching strategies, I will no longer dwell on them here, but, rather, I will close this chapter with Woolfolk's (1995) guidelines for educators who wish to establish affective programs. Woolfolk offers the following points for educators' considerations:

1. "Help students examine dilemmas they are currently

facing, or the dilemmas that they will face in the near future. This may include a discussion of prejudice, new students, or students with exceptional needs, for example. Teasing, intoxication, or conformity are some suggested topics for presentation by a facilitator.

2. Help students see others' perspectives--offer opportunities for role exchanges.

3. Help students make connections between expressed values and actions. Discuss situations. What should be done? How would you act? What would be your first step in this situation? What problems might arise?

4. Safeguard the privacy of all participants. Allow students to "pass" instead of answering certain questions. Don't allow peer pressure to force one to tell more than he wants to share.

5. Make sure students are really listening to each other. Use small groups. The teacher should also be a good listener.

6. Make sure as much as possible that the class reflects concern for moral issues. Distinctions should be evident between rules for administrative convenience (the orderly classroom) and rules based on moral issues. Favoritism of students and their responses should be avoided."[15]

These guidelines are applicable to all grade levels. Creative efforts with "more initiative and choice in the hands of the students" are recommended. Materials for classes need to be age appropriate, developmentally appropriate. The "traditional scheme of education including set plans, order, and demands" no longer has a positive impact on students. It is, rather, the well-monitored "open" plan which allows for the flexibility and genuine care that students need.[16]

Notes

1. G. Brown in *Human Teaching for Human Learning: An Introduction to Confluent Education,* 4-11.
2. Brown, op cit., 11.
3. Brown, op cit., 15-16.
4. D. Krathwohl, B. Bloom and B. Masia in *Taxonomy of Educational Objectives, Handbook II: Affective Domain,* 20.
5. D. Hamachek in *Human Dynamics in Psychology and Education: Selected Readings,* 379.
6. D. R. Halm in "The Affective Domain of Human Learning and Spiritual Instruction," 14.
7. Piaget is cited in Boesch, "The Development of Affective Schemata", 173-183.
8. J. Dressel in "Critical Thinking and the Perception of Aesthetic Form", 571.
9. Boesch, op cit., 173.
10. Hopefulness arises from natality--Arend, 1968 as cited in Elbaz.
11. I. Sonnier in "Holistic Education: Teaching in the Affective Domain", 11.
12. Sonnier, op cit.
13. G. Gazda, F. Asbury, F. Balzer, W.Childers, and R. Walters in *Human Relations Development,* 1.
14. R. Prawat in "Affective Versus Cognitive Goal Orientations in Elementary Teachers," 592.
15. A. Woolfolk in *Educational Psychology,* 92-93.
16. E. Johnson in *How to Live Through Junior High School,* 63.

References

Bayer, D. (1986). "The Effects of Two Methods of Affective Education on Self-Concept in Seventh Grade Students," The School Counselor, 34, 2.

Boesch, E. (1984). "The Development of Affective Schemata," Human Development, 27, 3-4.

Brown, G. (1986). *Human Teaching for Human Learning: An Introduction to Confluent Education.* England: Penguin Books.

Cobb, N. (1992). *Adolescence.* California: Mayfield Publishing.

Dressel, J. (1988). "Critical Thinking and the Perception of Aesthetic Form," Language Arts, 65, 6.

Elbaz, F. (1992). "Hope, Attentiveness, and Caring for Difference: The Moral Voice in Teaching," Teacher and Teacher Education, 8, 5-6.

Gazda, G., F. Asbury, F. Balzer, W. Childers, and R. Walters (1977). *Human Relations Development.* Boston: Allyn & Bacon.

Good, T.L. and J. E. Brophy (1977). *Educational Psychology: A Realistic Approach.* New York: Holt, Rinehart, and Winston.

Halm, D.R. (1995). "The Affective Domain of Human Learning and Spiritual Instruction," Unpublished paper.

Hamachek, D. (1972). *Human Dynamics in Psychology and Education: Selected Readings.* Boston: Allyn & Bacon.

Johnson, E. (1975). *How to Live Through Junior High School.* Philadelphia: J.P. Lippincott.

Krathwohl, D., B. Bloom, and B. Masia (1964). *Taxonomy of Educational Objectives, Handbook II: Affective Domain.* New York: McKay Co.

Prawat, R. (1985). "Affective Versus Cognitive Goal Orientations in Elementary Teachers" in American Educational Research Journal, 22, 4.

Sonnier, I. (1982). "Holistic Education: Teaching in the Affective Domain" Education, 103, 1.

Woolfolk, A. (1995). *Educational Psychology.* Boston: Allyn & Bacon.

CHAPTER 5
AN ASSESSMENT TOOL TO DETERMINE WHETHER YOU ARE AN AFFECTIVE TEACHER

I only met one teacher who I really believe did not like her students. It was the first day of classes at my new school, in my new position as guidance counselor. I happened to pull into the parking lot and leave my car at the same time as this teacher. We walked into the building together and she said to me, "I don't know why I'm even here. I hate kids!" I asked her why she was there. She told me she was too close to retirement to find a new career.

Except for this close-to-retiring teacher, I believe we are all affective teachers to some degree; we care about our students. Isn't that why we teach, after all? We all teach with the students' needs in mind.

This chapter will offer a means of assessing affectiveness. Because the affective domain is so difficult to measure, the degree of affectiveness that you self-ascribe is, definitely, a subjective call. (In preparation for Chapter 4 of my dissertation, I tried to measure the degree of teacher affect. The closest I could get was a label like "very affective" or "not-so-affective.") On the following pages you will find a kind of self-test including many questions that are based on suggestions of **STUDENTS**! Students' needs are in focus in any discussion of the affective domain and teaching. Why not listen to the students? These questions fall into one of three categories that are used to describe affectiveness among teachers-- **personality and attitude, the educational setting, and teaching methods**.

Please take a few minutes, in your own private time and in your own private space, to answer these questions about yourself. You may discover many affective qualities. And, even if you don't, you may accept the challenge to discuss your degree of affectiveness with others. Success breeds success. Wouldn't it be wonderful for our students if we, after realizing the importance of the affective domain, mentored and modeled affective behavior and implemented affective strategies into our teaching?

PERSONALITY and ATTITUDE

Are you friendly and outgoing toward your students?

Do you avoid roadblocks for the success of your students, and do you
   shape student success?

Do you treat each person as an individual?

Do you listen to and understand a student's life situation?

Are you happy to be teaching?

Do you smile often?

Are you patient?

Are you lenient when a situation calls for leniency?

Are you aware of your biases? (I had a student tell me once that he
   had no biases!)

Are you able to be non-judgmental?

Do you have a sense of humor?

Are you enthusiastic about your work?

Are you "young at heart?"

Are you able to empathize with students who are timid and who feel
   inferior?

Do you avoid favoritism?

Are you friendly in class and also friendly to students outside of
   class?

Are you able to understand that students have a life outside of school
   that includes other commitments such as family, job, etc.?

Are you able to "lighten up?"

Do you show concern for your students' progress (or lack of)
   THROUGHOUT the semester?

Do you really want to be a teacher?

Are you courteous?

Are you kind?

Do you model the Golden Rule? Are you respectful?

Do you treat all students with age appropriateness?

Are you able to forget negative experiences and move on rather than to hold
   students responsible for "historical events?"

Do you avoid talking down to your students?

Are you approachable, even in the hallway?

Do you avoid an air of superiority?

Are you in charge?

Do you believe that even though you're the teacher that students are able to
   communicate at the same level as you?

Do you avoid sarcasm?

Do you avoid intimidating behaviors?

Do you see the importance of changing "your way or the highway" to

a more democratic attitude?
Are you interested in your students as people?
Do you avoid distancing yourself from your students?
Are you a warm person? A loving person?
Are you able to express your emotions easily?
Are you truly concerned about the well-being of your students?
Are you aware of social issues?
Do you consider yourself to be emotionally stable?
Are you sympathetic, truthful, and compassionate?
Are you a good communicator?
Would your students say that you are not afraid to make AND admit
      errors?
Are you mature?

The EDUCATIONAL SETTING

Is there a conscientious effort to limit the number of students who can enroll
      for a course? Is the small classroom concept in focus?
Do you exhibit school/team spirit?
Are the walls of the classroom decorated?
Are there windows in the classrooms?
Do you use colors in the classroom--on the walls, especially?
Are there different over-the-lunch-hour programs offered for students?
Are you an advisor of one or several students?
Do you allow live animals or plants in your classroom?
Have you provided different learning centers?
Do you have neat JUNQUE in the classroom for the students to
      touch, assemble/disassemble, smell, listen to...?
Do you post student work--WITH PERMISSION?
Is your classroom clean?
Is your classroom the right temperature?
Is your classroom devoid of distracting noise for the majority of the
      day?
Is the library well-stocked?
Is your classroom complete with adequate reference materials? Would you
      allow for an over-stuffed chair in your back corner? A
      bathtub?
Do you dangle mobiles from the ceiling?
Do you allow soft music to be played at times?
Do you refrain from arranging students' desks in rows FOR THE

ENTIRE YEAR!!??!!

Are students allowed to move from their desks without permission?

Are students allowed to talk quietly with their friends?

Is your blackboard and your writing visible to all students?

If you use a podium or a lectern, are you able to step out in front of it
at times?

Do you move around the room?

Are you willing to give up your desk when students are present?!

Do you touch your students?

Do you usually speak in a normal tone of voice?

Is there adequate lighting in the classroom?

Do you believe in organized chaos?

Do you greet your students personally on a regular basis?

Are students allowed to wear jackets in the classroom? Hats?

Are backpacks allowed in the classroom? (Certainly these freedoms are
dictated by board policy.)

Is your building filled with student murals?

Do you provide frequent breaks for your students, especially when
they're involved in tedium?

Do you model unconditional positive regard for your students?

TEACHING METHODS

Do you allow students to ask questions?

Do you allow student discussions?

Are reviews for tests and quizzes offered to students?

Are you enthusiastic about your work?

Are you feeling "young at heart?"

Do you chat with your students--even about non-school events?

Do you use key notes on the board or on the overhead projector?

Do you monitor student work? Do you move around the classroom?

Do you allow a relaxed classroom setting?

Do you maintain high standards while integrating the curriculum?
(This may mean that you correct grammar in a psychology class!)

Do you deal with disciplinary problems effectively? What's
effective? Chapter 11 in *Educational Psychology*, Slavin.

Are you a life-long learner? Have you studied educational
psychology? (One of my children's teachers, who is a 20+ year
veteran, asked me to outline Slavin for him, to present course work
for him as a first time student of educational psychology. He

wanted to study during the regular school year.)

Are you clear and consistent in your objectives?

Do you allow for spontaneous activities?

Are you flexible?

Are you an effective lecturer? Lab instructor? Practicum supervisor? Learning at a distance coordinator? Do you incorporate affective strategies as presented in this book's chapters?

Do you offer suggestions to students, in particular, about how they might improve, about how they might be successful?

Do you continuously provide feedback, whether verbal or written?

Are you familiar with the schedules of reinforcement?

Do you avoid check-marking names to death in attempting to control behavior?

Do you allow more time for students who need it in order to complete a test/quiz?

Do you allow students to re-do assignments?

Do you offer verbal quizzes/tests to those who need them?

Are you able to pick up the pace in your presentation of information?

Are you a reflective teacher?

Do you read educational research?

Are you updated in developmental psychology?

Do you teach mnemonics?

Do you offer extra credit?

Do you collect student feedback/suggestions about your work and act on those suggestions in a timely manner?

Do you know students' names within a relatively short period of time?

Are you able to think at the level of a student?

Can you make the classroom a place where students want to be?

Are you prepared daily to teach?

Do you allow group work?

Are you able to integrate cooperative learning as prescribed by Slavin?

Do you realize that there is a difference between "group work" and "cooperative learning?"

Do you stop talking to check that your students are getting it?

Do you ask effective questions?

Do you allow wait time?

Do you rephrase a question before you answer your own question?

Do you randomly call on students?

Do you call on all students daily?

Do you wake students up when they doze? Do you maintain their wakefulness?

Do you know what the "proximal zone of development is?"

Do "A" students sometimes earn less than "A"s? (In my estimation, only a handful of "A" students will always receive "A"s if we are, in fact, challenging students according to their proximal zones of development.)

Is your teaching relevant to a student's daily living? Does the student perceive your teaching as relevant?

Do you assign reasonable amounts of homework?

Are you sure to work through a few assignment problems before the students leave your classroom?

Do you check, record, or discuss all work?

Do you consider the tossing of student work without using it a violation of Ed. Psych. 101?

Do you display student work with permission?

Do you hold high expectations of students?

Do you check for plagiarism?*

Do you teach different material to different sections of the same subject, especially if the students' needs dictate this?

Are you flexible in your presentation? Are you able to veer off on a tangent and regain your stance?

Do you facilitate class discussions?

Do you model respect?

Do you call on students by their first names?

Do you prohibit ethnic jokes in your classroom?

Do you treat each student fairly? Boys vs. girls?

Do you lecture with a sense of humor?

Is there a 10-minute time period available for independent practice?

Are you involved in corrective instruction?

Do you continuously check for mastery learning?

Have you revised "your way or the highway"attitude?

Do you refrain from tricking students, especially on quizzes or tests?

Do you extend time periods for assignments?

Do you review your presentation before allowing students to leave your classroom?

Do you use textbooks at grade level reading, ones with pictures, insets, testimonials?

Do you bring the learning down to the students' levels, if necessary?

Up to the students' levels?

Do you offer demonstrations? Explanations? Applications?

Do you review before you move on to a new concept?

Do you frequently engage students in hands-on activities?

Do you draw from students as resources?

Do you seek assistance at times from other resources within the building--the counselor, the special education teacher, the principal?

Do you offer both positive and negative comments to students?

Do you confer with your colleagues regarding just about everything?

Do you interact with your students daily?

Do you use simple language when presenting information?

Are assignments pertinent to the course of study?

Do you communicate with parents regularly?

Do you actively listen to your students?

Do you offer your students eye contact?

Do you listen to yourself on tape to determine whether practice will "fix" that monotone?

Have you developed "the look" that is so vital for disciplining, according to the principle of least intervention?

Do you focus on effort and not on ability?

Is it your responsibility to motivate students?

Do you monitor the probability of success and the incentive of work in order to motivate students?

Do you have a clear understanding of the different types of memory and, especially, the working of the long-term memory?

Do you engage in action research?

Do you have a bag of tricks to use to gain students' attention?

Do you fill in those few minutes at the end of class time with educational activities?

Do you start class on time? Are your students on time to class?

Are you available for your students? Do you offer them an e-mail address or another means of personally contacting you?

Do you strive to do your best for your students on a daily basis?

Do you protect and support students' rights?

ARE YOU PLEASED WITH MOST OF YOUR WORK AS A TEACHER?

If you have been able to answer in the affirmative to most of these questions--with minimal qualification--you are an affective teacher, to a degree. As you can see from these lists of questions, meeting students' needs is a relatively simple thing to do. Smiling, talking with students are usually natural behaviors. Yet, even a little bit of practice on even some of the natural behaviors will enhance the teacher's interaction with students. These questions are grounded in educational research. Not only have students of mine suggested these ideas as means for teachers to improve, but so have Slavin,Rogers,Good,Brophy, and other well-known educators/psychologists.

&&&&&&&&&&&&&&&&&&&&&&&&&&&&&&&&&&&&&&&&&

As an endnote, I need to comment on one of the questions that is listed as a characteristic of an affective teaching method--that of checking for plagiarism.* It seems that in this day and age of incredible technology, there is an overwhelming temptation for students to purchase or "borrow" written work from the Internet. Or, there may be sharing of papers among students from one semester to the other. I have taken a firm stand against plagiarism. I've also developed a reputation for being a "hard grader" because of it. I believe you can be a highly affective instructor while at the same time "holding the line." I will not lower my academic principles or standards because the student says this is the need. Rather, in a fashion similar to the "tough love" policy of the 70s, I will try in every way to help a student get through an assignment legitimately. I think we, as educators, are ethically bound to do this--maintain high standards and help students to achieve those standards. We can't excuse their falling short and give them points for completed work when it's interspersed with plagiarized text. A logical learning consequence of a lowered grade or failure is, definitely, in order. The "tough love" approach is still an affective strategy.

Good luck to you as you practice your affective strategies. I close in hopes of enhancing the positive teacher-student relationship which impacts a student's engagement in learning.